The Name of
the Beast

Also by Neil Taylor

In the Great Brand Stories series

Search Me: The surprising success of Google
(Cyan, 2005)

As an editor

From Here to Here: Stories inspired by London's Circle Line
Co-edited with John Simmons, Tim Rich and Tom Lynham
(Cyan, 2005)

As a contributor

26 Letters: Illuminating the alphabet
Edited by John Simmons, Freda Sack and Tim Rich
(Cyan, 2004)

Common Ground: Around Britain in 30 writers
Edited by John Simmons, Rob Williams and Tim Rich
(Cyan, 2006)

The Name
of the Beast

The perilous process of naming brands,
products and companies

Neil Taylor

First published in 2007 by:

Marshall Cavendish Limited
119 Wardour Street
London W1F 0UW
United Kingdom
T: +44 (0)20 7565 6000
F: +44 (0)20 7734 6221
E: sales@marshallcavendish.co.uk
Online bookstore: www.marshallcavendish.co.uk

and

Cyan Communications Limited
119 Wardour Street
London W1F 0UW
United Kingdom
T: +44 (0)20 7565 6120
E: sales@cyanbooks.com
www.cyanbooks.com

A CIP record for this book is available from the British Library

ISBN-13: 978-1-904879-70-1
ISBN-10: 1-904879-70-5

Printed and bound in Great Britain by
TJ International Ltd, Padstow, Cornwall

I thank you

To Sophie, Oisín and Suze for listening to me going on about word counts and deadlines. Again.

And to those ex-namers and still-friends who've gone on to better things ... Lou Dawson, Jeremy Faro, Arabella Scarisbrick, Rich Clayton, Laura Dixon, Laura Forman, Katya Williams and Yannis Kavounis.

Contents

The Name of
the Beast

1

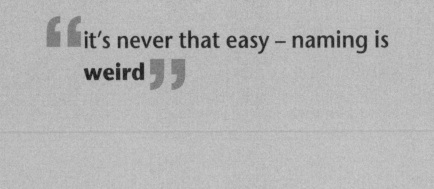

"it's never that easy – naming is **weird**"

Introduction: You're a what?

IT'S A GREAT LINE FOR PARTIES.

"Sorry, what was it you said you did?"

"I'm a namer."

"A what?"

"A namer. I think up names for things."

"Oh right. What … like for people's children?"

"No, for brands. Products or companies, that sort of thing."

"Oh, Right. I didn't know that job existed."

"Well, nor did I, until I got it."

"Wow. So what names have you thought of then?"

That's how it goes. Every time. Or it did, until I stopped being a namer for a living. Now, I work at language consultancy The Writer, where they let me write whole sentences, paragraphs, pages, heck, even a book or two. It can be hard work though. I've been trained to condense every idea into two words at most, often depending on a hilarious pun.

I was a namer, for four and a half years, at Interbrand, one of the world's biggest branding consultancies. Interbrand is the place that thought up names like Prozac, Expedia, Viagra, and Hobnobs (if you've never encountered that nobbly British biscuit, then you're missing a treat). I worked on names like Ocado (an online supermarket in the UK), *Intelligent Life* (a magazine for *The Economist*), and Jetix (the new name for the Fox Kids TV channel, which had to be renamed when Fox sold it to Disney).

Over the years, I've probably worked on hundreds of naming briefs (and thought up hundreds of thousands of names) for some of the biggest companies in the world. And I know you don't believe me, but it can be hard work. Admittedly, not like going down a mine or being sent up a chimney as a small child. But much harder work than you think. After all, naming sounds dead easy. Get a piece of paper, write down a few ideas, pick the best, and heigh-ho, time to go home.

Only it never is that easy. Naming is weird. Enemies are sent to test you. The names you think of that mean something negative – like "monkey murderer" in Mandarin. The names you think of that someone's already thought of (and sues you to stop you using). The names you think of that you can't get hold of the ".com" for. The names you think of that don't fit on the packaging. The truly brilliant names you think of that the client takes an irrational dislike to. The names you think of, that you just about persuade the client to go for, that get shot down in flames by punters in research groups. The names you come up with that the people who work for the company just laugh out loud at. The names you come up with that the press ridicule. The names you come up with that manage to antagonize your customers so much that they stop buying your product until you change it. These have all happened to brand names (but not necessarily, I hasten to add, to names I've come up with).

All of these have happened at one time or another. There's just so much to go wrong. OK, I can't pretend it's all hard work. In fact, what an amazing job to get! Fresh out of university, and someone tells you they'll pay you – actual real money! – to loll about thinking up words. But there is more to it than meets the eye.

Naming is in fact one of the hardest marketing jobs you'll ever do. No, trust me. Everyone feels qualified to stick their oar in – after all, we can all speak, so we all have an opinion on words and sounds – and lots of people have named their children. Only no parent ever got sacked for choosing a stupid name for their child, although clearly some should be: Paris Hilton, anyone? And few of us have to worry about how our children's names are going to go down on the other side of the world, or if we're going to wind up all the people who already have that name. It's not just your colleague you'll be answerable to, but your customers and the media.

So in this book, we'll look at the nuts and bolts of how you go about coming up with a name. How do you get the brief right? What sort of name should you go for? What makes a good name? How do you make sure it doesn't mean anything awful in another language? How do you make sure someone else isn't using it? More importantly, why do people care so much about such a little thing, anyway? We'll look at the odd little human bits of coming up with a name. Who should you involve? Should you ask your customers what they think? How do you convince people you've picked a good name? What do you do if the newspapers poke fun at it? Or worse, what about if your customers hate the name?

Imagine my surprise – I nearly choked on my cornflakes in fact – when in the middle of writing this book, I opened up my morning paper to find this rant by Andrew Mueller, writing in the *Guardian* about my former profession:

There are people, enviable yet contemptible, who make good livings inventing names for companies. That is, over-funded start-ups or insecure established operations with more money than imagination approach these brand consultants, as they're known, give them a skipful of cash, and in return receive a new corporate identity, almost always a zany misspelling or fatuous neologism. It's nice work if you can get it. In fact, if you're a CEO about to shovel a five-figure fee at some twit called Nathan to come up with a name like Twerq or Zamp Plus or X-Zite!, get in touch – for half the money, I'll do you something at least as good, and certainly no more foolish.

One name in particular gets singled out for attack, the UK mobile phone retailer Phones4U:

It's easy to imagine how Phones4U got themselves into this pickle. When the guilty party thought of the name, they doubtless believed they'd triumphed on two levels. Phones4U has a does-what-it-says-on-the-tin integrity ("Phones") and a cutting-edge text abbreviation aspect ("4 U"). What they didn't realise was that they'd failed on two levels. Calling your phone company "Phones" is like calling your dog "Dog" – it doesn't distinguish yours from anyone else's. Adding the "4 U" is declaring yourself the intellectual kin of a 14-year-old texting his gormless mates about which McDonald's to meet in.

   ... At the risk of diverting further money into the pockets of some unctuous logo-peddling cowboy, nothing less than a complete image overhaul will do. Or there's the cheaper option, outlined above. The address to write to, by happy coincidence, is below.

You see, people do really care about names. Why? Once you've worked out the answer to that you still need to come up with the name. Do you really need to hand over megabucks to a gang of brand consultants in black-rimmed specs, or should you just do it yourself? And why are there sharp-suited lawyers so intent on walking off with even more of your hard-earned marketing budget?

We might even get to talk about a few of the great names I loved, and which I tried to sell to clients again and again, but which for some reason, no one ever bought. Here's a sneak preview: World On Toast, Forty Blinks, Canopy, Not Grey, Shocking Beige, Unperhaps. Their time will come.

2

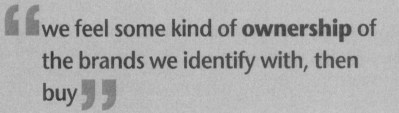

"we feel some kind of **ownership** of the brands we identify with, then buy"

Who cares?

MY EXPERIENCE AT PARTIES PROVED TO ME PEOPLE
WERE interested in naming. But I was surprised at just how much. It doesn't just apply to young professional partygoers. I know from the amount of media coverage we used to get at Interbrand about naming that the public must be interested, too. Why? People don't seem to feel quite the same about logos, or straplines. What is it about a name that fascinates us?

The first answer is the link between names and identity. Take our own names. I'm not that fussed about Neil, or my middle name Michael, but I do like my surname. It's somehow important that I'm a Taylor. Would I be the same person if I weren't a Taylor? Or a Neil Michael? Of course, I'll never know. But it means we understand personally how a fairly arbitrary set of letters can come to represent something much more subtle and sophisticated. When I asked Síne (pronounced Sheena) Old, of brand consultancy Dave, what her favourite name is, she said:

My name – it perfectly captures what I stand for. It's slightly different and fresh to listen to, it has an element of cheekiness in the first three letters, is logically grounded in mathematics like my mind, whilst being culturally aligned to my heritage.

OK, Síne has her tongue firmly in her cheek, but there's an element of truth there, especially on the last point since Síne is Irish. We imbue names – especially our own – with stories and sets of associations.

That's exactly what brand names do too. They are a form of shorthand. Brand names that work instantly trigger the associations of the brand (hopefully good ones). Jeff Bezos, founder of Amazon, said, "A brand is what people say about you when you're not in the room." And a lot of that is enshrined in the name. Because your name is the primary means of identification for a brand, this wee little thing is arguably the most important element of the branding mix. Brands change logo, strapline, headquarters, people – some of them even dramatically change what they do (Nokia started off making forestry products and rubber boots). But often the name is the one common thread that runs throughout the entire history of a company or product. So most hope never to change the name. That means that when brands do change name, it's a big deal.

What I've said explains why companies care about their names, and why the rest of us are interested. But often we're not just interested. We're angry, outraged even. Why on earth does it matter to us?

I think there are two things going on. First, most of us choose to buy brands we like (or at least the brands we like more than others). Some people's willingness to shave the Nike swoosh into their heads prove that they're not just picking Nike because they feel it makes the most efficient sports footwear.

Indeed, many Nike buyers never get within a mile of a basketball court or a running track. Their choice of the Nike brand is saying something that's not just functional, but emotional. It is saying something about their own identity.

The second reason is just familiarity. Many products, and their names, become as much as part of everyday speech as words like car, table or cat. Some brand names – like Google and Hoover – even make it into the category of true everyday vocabulary. With words like car, table or cat, no one tells us that those are the right words to use. We just sort of know. And because they are equally owned by all of us, no one can really change them (unless we all want them to change).

Not surprisingly then, we feel some kind of ownership of the brands we identify with, then buy, and the names we use for them. They become familiar, dependable parts of our lives. Sometimes they become so much a part of our lives that we end up giving brands nicknames, like we might with our friends. Think of Coke, Bud, Merc, Beemer, or the numerous nicknames for McDonald's across the world: Mickey D's in the US, MacDo in France, Macky D's in the UK. It's as if we feel we know them so well we have the right to "pet" them. This shortening of brand names, and the familiarity and identification it symbolizes, is a holy grail for namers. But it's difficult to engineer, because it's down to so much more than just the name. The best the namer can hope to do is come up with the sort of name that's easy to play with, and hope that the whole brand package connects with its target customers.

So when a brand decides to changes its name, it's a bit disconcerting. Because we feel we own the names to some extent, it's a bit annoying that a brand can unilaterally decide to change the name. Naturally, they feel it's theirs to change – from their point of view, it's a mere bit of intellectual property they own, and theirs to do with as they please.

But in one sense, the public has a power of veto. Because if we're very unhappy with a name change, we can make a big fuss, by writing to the company, or writing to the press. And if it really means that much to us, we can stop doing business with the perpetrator. We could even stop handing over our cash.

In the UK, there's been furore after hullaballoo after stink. When Opal Fruits became Starburst. When Marathon became Snickers. (Snickers, by the way was the name of Mr Mars's horse. Mr Mars being the man who started Mars, naturally.) When Oil of Ulay became Olay. When Jif became Cif. Most of these have been done by large multinationals for reasons of international scale. The products have ended up with different names in different territories. Bringing them all into line helps you reduce marketing costs, packaging costs, and the like, because you can attempt to make one size fit all.

Sometimes a name change causes a real fuss. See the reaction on the BBC website when the UK's Post Office group changed its name to Consignia:

Consignia doesn't sound like the national institution that Royal Mail does. Instead, it reminds me of that brand of anti-perspirant, called Insignia. I also think it sounds dreadfully 80s, and therefore just a bit naff.
Jonathan Talbot, UK

Having just come back from holiday I noticed that Consignia means lost luggage in Spanish – how appropriate is that?
Melanie, UK

Call it T-mail. A modern competitor to E-mail. T stands for terra, as in earth as opposed to electronic. If they use this then I would

expect as much money from it as the clowns that thought up Consignia.
Robert Tiffney, UK

Unfortunately they obviously forgot that a more common use of "consign" is to consign to history, consign to the rubbish bin ... more a term of throwing away than taking care of. They should throw away their dictionaries and think about how real people actually use language. Royal Mail has a huge history and therefore degree of trust. Whether a royalist or republican one can't forget a hundred years of service. Do we want to throw away these "real" words in favour of some meaningless fudge of dictionary definitions?
Gabriel, UK

Still can't see what's wrong with the old name GPO (General Post Office). Or, in the US, they call theirs US Mail – what about UK Mail? Keep It Simple, Stupid.
M. Drazin, UK

It's a poor excuse to say that Royal Mail could be confusing when it takes a paragraph to explain what Consignia means.
Emma Taylor, UK

Simple. Call it "The Post Office" or "Royal Mail." Retain its British identity. British Airways operates overseas by definition, and possibly the worst thing it did recently was to repaint its aircraft to disguise its British-ness, which was arguably its greatest asset.
Andrew Wilson, UK

Given the current crisis within the Post Office, Consignia Plc seems like an excellent name. It is an anagram of Panic Closing.
Howard Morris

It should be renamed "Resignia," as the name ingeniously includes the key word "resign". I have extensively market researched this brand (with my next door neighbour's pet budgie) and I am pleased to report that it has met with an approval rating

of 110%. My invoice for £1,000,000 consultancy is now in the
post ready to arrive at your desk first thing next week for your
approval. Yours sincerely, St. George Brands.
Roland, UK

Dementia.
Martyn, UK

Con What? Just because other companies change their name,
it doesn't mean that you have to change Royal Mail and Post
Office.
Ken Ellis, UK

There was nothing – and is nothing – wrong with "Royal Mail."
Keep the name and keep it in public ownership.
Richard Brennan, UK

My comments are largely unprintable but ... my experience of
management is people who can't do anything useful, wasting
money and resources that should be going to people that actually
do something useful. Angry medical advisor – insurance.
Louisa Morgan, UK

What's wrong with "The Royal Mail?" Overseas they will just
have to think up a jazzy brand "look." E.g. That bright red
colour and font etc they use over here. Even though some might
think "Royal Mail" might be confusing, considering how much
recognition *The Times* has as a newspaper internationally, and
how much people know of the British Royal family overseas,
"The Royal Mail" will ring true with foreign people's image of
England.
J. Lee, UK

The Post Office, always was, is, and should remain our property,
to serve our purposes. If it is losing money, then we should
rationalize it, or update its systems, or maybe the cost of letters
should be raised. The last thing that should happen is that
it becomes yet another vehicle for investor speculation and
profit-chasing. The name Consignia (just like Accenture and

all the other pretentious self-aggrandizing names) makes me immediately think of insincerity.
Blewyn, UK

The Post Office has pretty much proved that they are not competent to expand internationally so there's no problem. Stick to Royal Mail.
Merlin Magee, UK

Don't dump your history and heritage ... There is nothing wrong with Royal Mail. In Australia we don't even have proper buildings for post offices, they have all been sold off. Instead we have sub-agents in lotto shops and newsagents. All sense of trust and reliability has flown out the window. I love your post offices and the fact that you have a Royal Mail. Maybe I am nostalgic but I am probably not the only one.
Michael Bowden, Australia

You see, we really do care. We'll come back to this in Chapter 6. Consignia has now been consigned to history as a massive failure. Another name change that went backwards in the UK was Kellogg's attempt to turn the breakfast cereal Coco Pops to Choco Krispies.

If you announce your name change on a slow news day, you're in trouble. The media take enormous pleasure in whipping up a storm around what is probably mild irritation among the public. Of course, naming is an easy target for the media. The product of a naming process is just a few letters. But as the Consignia response shows, it is the carrier for a ton of emotional associations. It's therefore very easy to find big criticisms of a little name which could never hope to keep everyone happy. Coupled with that, naming processes are usually associated with more dramatic rebranding exercises. Cue the ridicule of lying consultants, and outrage at the amount of money they get paid. The media is always talking about the cost of renaming processes, and hugely over-inflating it. No naming job in my experience has ever cost much more than a couple of hundred thousand US dollars, mostly spent on legal fees. But the price the media quotes is usually in the millions – figures which have usually included redesigning a logo, and then applying it to stationery, buildings, vehicles, uniforms, and the cost of advertising and PR to launch the new brand. But most of these are costs these businesses would have incurred even if they hadn't rebranded, so the figures are decidedly unfair.

The moral of the story is just that naming is a tricky beast. It looks easy, but can have big consequences at each step of the process. So the first step of the process is to do some good hard thinking before you even start coming up with nice-sounding words.

3

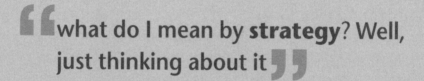

"what do I mean by **strategy**? Well,
just thinking about it**"**

Diff'rent strokes

SO, YOU NEED A NAME.

Before you sit there with your flipchart and your glass of slightly nasty red wine, thinking of the first name that comes into your head, you need to decide what sort of name you want. This is not like naming your child, where you can just leaf through a list of names that already exist, and say, "How about that?" "Won't she get bullied at playschool if we call her Peaches?" Or "Over my dead body!" with an increasingly frustrated loved one.

No. This is a question of that hatefully ubiquitous business mantra, strategy. Ideally when you say this word you should be sipping a takeaway Starbucks cappuccino and rolling the word *stradddegy* into your mobile with the most insincere mid-Atlantic drawl you can muster. What do I mean by strategy? Well, just thinking about it. Different types of names do different kinds of jobs, and have different implications, so it makes sense to think about all this stuff before you start.

Descriptive names

The simplest sorts of names are descriptive. In the words of a famous British TV commercial, they do exactly what they say on the tin. Things like British Airways, Canadian Tire and Deutsche Bank.

Not surprisingly, this is how naming started. Tell people what it is, and they'll buy it, won't they? The good news about descriptive names is that they're cheap to promote. Because the name is so easy to understand, you could probably launch the product or service without spending too many millions of dollars on an advertising campaign just to explain what it is. But these types of name have many downsides, too. Firstly, they're only descriptive in one language. If you don't speak English, and you see the name British Airways, then British won't mean very much to you and nor will Airways. The simplest, most elegant name in one language can become an ugly, incomprehensible load of rubbish in another.

These names might have a geographical constraint, but they can also restrict you in terms of what the brand actually offers. Be too descriptive about your wares and you may find your name starts to look quaint as life moves on. A few years ago, Lastminute.com launched in a blaze of PR glory in the UK, offering cheap last minute holidays. And their name helped them get their message over quickly. But think what happens a few years down the line. What happens if they want to sell holidays you book six months in advance? Their name might well hold them back.

One of the UK's biggest mobile phone retailers is called The Carphone Warehouse. Clearly, it's a business that was named when cellular phones were in their infancy, and mainly found in cars (largely because they were the size of bricks and so bloody heavy that you really needed an engine to help transport you round). And Carphone Warehouse started off selling out of outlets something like warehouses. Of course, times change. Now carphones don't exist, and Carphone Warehouse sells out of wee shops on Britain's high streets just like any other retailer. If you think about it, their name now seems a little odd and outdated (but not quite old-fashioned enough to be quaint). Indeed, as they've spread across Europe they've used the name The Phone House. Is the fact that their name has been left behind a problem? Not really, it seems, but I suspect that they are now a familiar enough brand in Britain that we've just stopped thinking about the literal meaning of the name. And because they've made their brand stand for more than just what they do; they're also known for a friendly, independent, humorous, approach, which is now probably the primary set of associations when we hear the name.

One way around the problem, when your name gets superseded by events, is to turn your name into a set of initials which are then immune to the ravages of time. So International Business Machines became IBM, General Electric Company became GEC, Wire and Paper Products became media giant WPP and British retailer Asda morphed out of the Associated Dairies. The *Korea Times* recently reported on the tendency for Korean companies to switch to initials:

Kudos to the LG Group! Its trade name used to be Lucky-Goldstar for many years until 1995 when they adopted the new name, LG, as part of its strategy to project a more modern and friendlier image. On the heels of their successful handling of the corporate brand identity in the domestic market, its flagship LG Electronics is now aggressively pitching its brand name in overseas markets, including the US.

But a set of initials is definitely a fix. If you've got the option, it makes sense to start off with a name that leaves you enough scope for your business to change without hamstringing you in terms of what you can do, or forcing you to change the name. I've always been amazed by brands that launch under a set of initials. After all, a name is usually an opportunity to say something about yourself – either what you do, or the way you do it. Initials say nothing, and tend to be anonymous and difficult to remember. Tom Blackett, group deputy chairman of Interbrand, says in an article on Brandchannel:

Initials are perhaps the most difficult form of brand name in which to create meaning. They tend, almost entirely, to be business rather than product brand names, and are used by organizations that are confident they will be understood – like IBM and ICI – or who are happy to shelter under relative anonymity (LG, for example). The truth is that very few companies or products would choose the initials route if they were new to the market. Initials lack information, differentiation and personality; they are also notoriously difficult to protect as trademarks.

Brands that launch under initials usually suggest to me a political fight internally – they can't agree on what they want to say, so they choose the inoffensive but short-sighted option they can agree on.

Descriptive names, though, are relatively hard to protect as trademarks, unless you've been around for years and years. That's because trademark law is there, in theory, at least, to prevent ordinary – and simple – punters like you and me from getting confused. So, with a brand new name, you're not allowed to trademark any words that are deemed descriptive of the product. That's because it would be unfair on your competitors. If you made orange juice, and someone let you trademark the name "Orange" for that product, anyone else making orange juice would be pretty scuppered, really. Marketing their product would be like playing taboo (sorry, Taboo™), desperately trying to describe something without using the most obvious word for it.

But because really descriptive names are the most obvious way of getting functional information across, and people have been picking names like that for centuries, many of them got into use – and the public consciousness – a long time before trademarks appeared. So the lawyers cut them some slack. If you can prove that your name – however descriptive – is famous enough that most people know it, you can use that as a defence against competitors "passing off" their products or services as yours. Again, it's to protect little old us from thinking that one person's shoddy knock-off products are really the super-duper ones we know and love.

All this doesn't mean that your descriptive name need end up being completely anonymous and rip-offable. When British Airways launched their low cost airline they called it Go, just the sort of name to get a trademark lawyer twitchy. Was it descriptive? Why shouldn't a competitor be allowed to use the word "go" to describe an airline (and if not in the name, then at least in the marketing that supports it)? Well, fair point. So, to make Go distinctive, British Airways had to register the name in conjunction with its logo – the word in a lower case, sans serif type in a circle. So it was the name and visual identity which were protected together. Competitors were allowed to use the word 'go', but not in a way that made it look too confusingly like the original version. Of course, it's possible that over time British Airways could have argued that the name had become so well known that it deserved protection in its own right. We'll never know. Stelios Haji-Ioannou came along with easyJet, some big orange planes, and a wad of cash. BA sold him Go, and their polka dot planes were no more.

Image-based names

The next set of names work in a different way. Where descriptive names are entirely literal – describing what you're going to get – image-based names work by association, in that they compare one thing to another. Visa is a classic example. A Visa card is not literally a visa – try presenting it at passport control and you won't get very far (a few unscrupulous South American countries excepted). But if a loved one is kind enough to take you shopping somewhere exotic, then your Visa card might feel a bit similar, giving you access to products and places, smoothing your way around the commercial world.

Lots of image-based names are essentially metaphors – they compare something to something else, usually something more familiar. Visa is a relatively straightforward one. When I was working with the branding agency Coley Porter Bell in London, we came up with a Teleport – a name for a service that sends the TV programmes you want to watch down a cable to your house, whenever you want. It sounded to us as if it might feel like the sort of thing you read about or see in a science fiction novel or film, transporting you instantly to a different world. It sounded like a teleport. Essentially the name works as a mnemonic, a shortcut to a much bigger story. Indeed that's often how the best names work; they're shorthand for something bigger, a set of associations you can explore through the rest of your marketing.

But these metaphors don't need to just refer to how a product works, or its benefit to your life. It might connect to the feeling they want you to have about the brand. Phone company

Orange has nothing to do with colours or fruits, but they do want you to think of the brand and these things sharing a few qualities – freshness, vividness, a sense of vitality.

And these image-based names don't even have to be real words. With some names, we pick up on resonances in the sounds of names; they cue up thoughts of other words in our heads. Think of Viagra. Not a real word, but echoes of Niagara, and the word for "life" in lots of Romance languages. Which is one of the main pros of these kinds of names; you can pick a word, or hint at words, that travel – words that might be common to lots of different languages. It gets you over part of the linguistic barrier that holds back the descriptive names. To a large extent, this has meant that names which play on Latin or Greek roots, with echoes in Modern European languages, have long been the bread and butter of the naming industry. Tom Blackett says:

Associative names have become the "lingua franca" of international branding. Because they are relatively easy to understand, they simplify the task of positioning the product or service concerned, and therefore, they allow the advertiser the luxury of developing "brand personality," thus strengthening differentiation at an emotional level.

But of course, these names have a drawback too. In any category, the most obvious metaphors and associations can be overused. How many brands are there called Apex, Pinnacle, Focus, and the like? That's true even of the classical roots underlying many of the names too, to the point where new names like Centrica and Consignia can seem simultaneously familiar and anonymous. Obvious images not only become bland and hackneyed, but they get harder to register, too, as everyone fights over the same ideas.

These names also come with a financial impact. They cost more. Not to create, or register, or protect, but to market. After all, if your name doesn't say exactly what you do, you need to spend time, space and money explaining what you *do* do before you've even started convincing me that your trainers, widgets, or mortgages are better than someone else's. So why would you bother? Well, in theory, because they start to imbue your brand with more emotional associations than a descriptive name. There's something warmer, more imaginative about them. They have more personality. And that's the point of a brand after all: to add an emotional element to a decision – to buy or not to buy – that most of us like to believe is purely functional and rational.

Abstract names

The last big category is the names that have no relation whatsoever to the product or service they label. Think of something like Kodak, or Xerox. These are names we've grown used to, but which must have seemed like the oddest thing out when they first appeared on the scene. The story (probably apocryphal) goes that George Eastman, the founder of Kodak, liked Ks. He thought they were unusual, and cool. So, when thinking what to call his company, he stuck a K at the beginning, a K at the end, and found some stuff to go in the middle to make it sound like a word.

Why just make up a name, when you could pick something ready-made and loaded with resonances and meaning? Well there's a clue in Eastman's thinking – that Ks were unusual. A made-up name guarantees you there'll be nothing else like it. Unique. Not only that – and by now, I'm sure you're one step ahead of me – a truly unique name is a trademark lawyer's dream. Something that doesn't look or sound like anything else is a really easy name to register and protect. That's why some of the busiest trademark categories – like pharmaceuticals and computer-related stuff – read like *The Lord of the Rings*. To get your trademark through, you'll need to find something really weird.

Which is part of the problem. A really abstract name can seem very alien; there's nothing much for us to get hold of, no emotion to piggyback into your brand. Abstract names – especially the scientific ones, full of Xs, Zs and Qs – can feel very cold because they're so deliberately different. When they don't work, they're horrible.

But when they do, you get something quite special. The branders call these names "empty vessels" because they don't carry any meaning beyond the brand. You can make these words stand for exactly what you want, without the pesky reality of actual oranges and visas getting in the way. Hear Kodak or Xerox enough and they're utterly unique, utterly memorable, and utterly synonymous with their products. Blackett says:

Abstract names are potentially strong marketing and legal properties. They can create powerful differentiation, which, if backed up by products and services of high quality and value for money, can lead to strong and successful brands.

There's a question here, though, about how abstract any name really is. Some would argue that even the most extraordinarily odd names still carry some resonances, just because of the sounds they use. In fact, some people sell names based on the "sound symbolism" of the letters that make them up. The existence of sound symbolism is something that academic linguists have been arguing about for years. Some of the evidence is initially quite convincing. Think how many English words for a slightly unpleasant slipperiness start with an "sl": slip, slide, slither, slough, slink. The problem is that there are so many words in any language and, relatively, so few sounds, that it's easy to jump on patterns and ignore the evidence of thousands of words that contradict them. Take the "i" sound in little, titchy, imp. Is it the sound we use to suggest smallness? Some have said so, but it turns up in the word "big" too. Oh dear. Andy McCrum, of naming consultants Appella is a big supporter of sound symbolism, but even he admits, "It's dependant on the phonology of the language. A powerful, strong p isn't much good in a language without a p in its phonological canon such as Arabic."

What is certain is that in marketing terms, theses names are really expensive to launch and support. After all, they really give no clue as to what the hell a brand is going to be about. And they're often initially really unpopular, purely because they are so self-consciously disconnected from the real world. When British chemicals giant ICI announced it was going to hive off its pharmaceuticals business into a separate company, and that it was going to be called Zeneca, one media analyst said that it would be the "biggest act of commercial suicide" in history. And of course, in the first few weeks of the business being renamed, people there did find it odd answering the phone with such an unlikely mouthful. But as with any name, because the company stuck with it, people got used to it pretty quickly. And the act of commercial suicide? For a long time after the demerger, ICI shares plummeted as Zeneca shares rose.

Names of provenance

There's another obvious class of names, which although theoretically "abstract" – bearing no relation to the thing being sold – has strong associations with where the product comes from, or the history of the company that produces them; their provenance, in short. These are people's names or place names. People's names are probably the most common single class of name – McDonald's, Ford, Cadbury. Nearly half of the world's top 100 brands in Interbrand's league table of the most valuable brands use family names. Tom Blackett says:

Many of the family names are concentrated in such sectors as finance (Merrill Lynch, Morgan Stanley, Goldman Sachs) and fashion (Louis Vuitton, Gucci, Chanel), but they are to be found in most industries, as Mercedes-Benz, Gillette, Kellogg's, Pfizer, Harley-Davidson, Wrigley, Hertz, and Heineken show. They are spread across industries and are by no means confined to "smokestack" or "heritage" businesses. They tend to be associated with products and services where the personal touch and continuity over the years are both seen as important. Authenticity is therefore an important attribute that family names help express. Perhaps the lesson here is that family names can be most effective in areas where the product or service is innovative and unfamiliar, and where consumers need that extra degree of reassurance to buy for the first time. The presence of a personal endorsement in the brand name (and therefore the implied accountability) can provide the trust that is needed to prompt the purchase decision.

These names, like other abstract names, act as something of an empty vessel. As Martin Lee, co-founder of branding and research agency Acacia Avenue, says:

Very shortly into the life of a company, the name has no independent life from its products or its reputation. Take Dyson for instance. Its name is simply the name of its owner, and immediately after launching, that's all it would have meant, and if you know nothing of James Dyson, it gave you nothing at all. But now, everyone has a clear sense of what Dyson stands for, in terms of innovation and product performance. Many people will know of the founder, but it's becoming less important as time goes by. And many names have lost all their meaning, other than that which customers ascribe to them. For instance, who knows what MFI stands for?

Many products – especially food – carry the names of their home towns or regions – Parma ham, Lancashire cheese, champagne. Often names of provenance are the stuff of legal battles. Often local producers try to prevent the use of the name on products made outside a local region, almost the equivalent of the *appellation contrôlée* you get in French wine regions. But many less tangible products and services are named according to their starting points, like the UK bank Halifax, or car brand Vauxhall.

Retail chains are often based on the founders' names: Marks & Spencer, Zellers, Tim Hortons. It's so expected of supermarket names in the UK – with brands like Sainsbury's and Budgen's – that we even add that apostrophe "s" to names that were never anybody's name, leaving things like Tesco's (which was started by a Mr Cohen) and Asda's (which, as we've seen, started off life as the Associated Dairies, and is now "part of the Wal-Mart family" as they say in their delightfully homespun way).

There's also a great rule of thumb when using people's names. One name, and you're middle of the road: Littlewoods, Ford. Two names, and you're slightly, or even a lot, posher: Fortnum & Mason, Rolls-Royce, Dean & Deluca. Three names, you're a law firm: Freshfields Bruckhaus Deringer, Field Fisher Waterhouse. Four names (the less pronounceable the better), with egos running riot, and you can only be an advertising agency: Euro RSCG Wnek Gosper. Even though these names are abstract, their structure now actually hints at their category.

Orange

Ask the namers what they think is the best brand name, and Orange comes up again and again (like it does in this book). Mathew Weiss of Coley Porter Bell says Orange is a great name:

Because it broke the norms of the category and is a good example of the "Pip Principle." In *Great Expectations* Pip is born a no one with nothing; his name reflects this. But through strength of character he grows into a man of substance. What's in a name is merely the sum of what you make of it. Who in their right mind would name a cleaning product Fairy for instance?

Orange's category breaking is reinforced by Landor's David Gaglione, who says:

When creating names, it's important to consider competitor names. An ideal name is one that is differentiated (and relevant). Orange – certainly at the time of launch – was highly differentiated and very unexpected. It signals something new in a stagnant market – it motivates people to notice the name and, in many ways, motivates people to be part of it. We know that imagery fires the imagination and increases recall. Selecting a colour certainly fires the imagination and leaves an imprint in one's mind. The name Orange selected provides a platform for them to tell an interesting story – change and excitement.

OK, OK, we get it. You love it. What few people know is that Hutchison, Orange's original daddy, tried to launch a mobile brand once before, under the similarly category-breaking name Rabbit – "to rabbit" is cockney slang for "to talk." But it didn't work. So is the success of Orange a case of 20/20 naming hindsight?

A spectrum of names

While it's easy to find these broad categories of names, they're not entirely discrete. They bleed into each other at the edges. Names like I Can't Believe It's Not Butter are treading the line between being descriptive and more image based. Both descriptive names and image-based names can be based on real words or invented ones: a name like Microsoft is made up, but from fairly descriptive elements; Vodafone is simply made up of the elements voice, data and phone. An invented name like Häagen-Dazs may seem abstract to some; to others it might evoke some sophisticated European provenance. Indeed, sometimes brand new brands use real names to evoke an entirely spurious heritage, like Bailey's Irish Cream liqueur, or Caffrey's beer, two apparently authentic Irish products, both dreamed up in a marketing brainstorm.

So how do you decide which you want? Well, sometimes you need to try to come up with some names of each type before it really becomes clear which will work best. That decision will always come down to something of a balancing act between different factors. David Gaglione, associate director of naming and strategy at Landor in the US, says:

Firing an emotion or generating a reaction is the single best measure of a name. This is typically achieved by creating names that are differentiated in their space (stand out), relevant (mean something to key audiences) and tell a story about the brand.

Tom Blackett says:

Your first duty is to the customer, because if you look after the customer, as the saying goes, the business will look after itself. This means that you must strike the right balance between explaining what the new product is about, and creating differentiation to secure future purchaser loyalty. It is the role of advertising to explain features and benefits as the first phase in any new product launch; it is the role of the name to capture this information and to provide the platform for developing brand personality. It is perhaps no coincidence that two of the fastest growing brands in the world – Samsung and Apple – have abstract names. They both have excellent products, and this is the most important factor. But their names, which are highly distinctive and memorable, provide an extra competitive edge, and in crowded marketplaces this can make all the difference.

Both Gaglione and Blackett focus on differentiation as crucial to naming success, and I agree. After all, naming, like branding in general, is there to give people a reason to choose your brand over other people's. In fact, Alex Batchelor, director of marketing at the Post Office in the UK, used to say, "Brands are there to rescue people from the tyranny of choice." You do that by standing out from the competition, and being remembered. That's why one of the simplest naming rules of thumb is to pick the opposite type of name to your main competitors if you can. Sometimes whole sectors of business are full of brands with similar types of names. Brands that enter those categories with a different sort of name – let's call them category breakers – often do well. It's a theme we'll come back to in this book, as most of my favourite names are exactly that.

4

"the problem; companies not being able to find anything that is **different** to say about themselves"

Dedicated followers of fashion

DESPITE ALL THE RIGOUR AND LOGIC WE NAMERS TRY to impose on our odd little discipline, we can't help being buffeted by our own likes and dislikes, and even the whims of fashion.

Glyn Britton of the communications agency Albion says:

I have a penchant for classic American product brand names from the first half of the 20th century. I like names like La-Z Boy and Play-Doh, although I think my favourite has to be Yo-Yo, which was trademarked by Duncan in 1929. These names are so obviously mangled in order to be trademarkable that they develop a special charm of their own, but they are also honest; they look like brand names. They have all also come to be used generically, which I think is a mixed blessing. It lessens their commercial success, but is perhaps the ultimate cultural approval.

Ever since I joined the naming business in the late 1990s, there have been trends that have come and gone. The early 1990s were all about what I call the "Euroschlapp" corporate names, seemingly designed by lawyers, or computers, or computerized lawyers, made up of spurious Latin or Greek roots. There are tons of them: Diageo, Consignia, Syngenta and the like. The naming spirit of the 1990s in brand agencies like Landor, Interbrand and Nomen is brilliantly spoofed by the website www.enormicom.com:

Nametron 3000™

Enormicom's patented **Nametron 3000™** uses a complex system of algorithms and formulas to combine morphemes, phonemes and gigonemes to create a Singular Cohesive Action Moniker (S.C.A.M.®) for your company. The result is a truly best of breed name that conveys the essence of your brand's soul.

It then goes on to list (real) corporate brand names the device has spewed out:

Lucent
Scient
Viant
Teligent
Naviant
Noviant
Novient
Aquent
Livent
Omnient
Luminant
Cerent
Agilent
Sapient
Vivant
Ravisent

Last time I visited the site, I got Similant. It then goes on to design an equally generic logo for your new brand based on the nondescript arc so many companies use. The problem of the bland name and logo both come down to the same thing; companies not being able to find anything that is different to say about themselves (or not having the confidence to focus on the things that do make them different). Martin Lee says:

The worst examples of this are all those high tech company names that are full of neologisms all aimed at sounding different, which in fact all end up sounding identical. All the following are genuine company names of the last ten years: Inprise, Acxiom, Elementis, Virage, Derivium, Sopheon, Numis, Enodis, Spirent, Trimeris, and Veos. All these namers have been hitting the random word generator button. Incidentally, I've got something I must show you from the Fourth Room (his former agency). We did a satirical piece of marketing called Brand Flakes, from which this list is taken. It was a rip off of a Kellogg's box, with all the flaky brands included.

Diageo is absolutely typical of this kind of branding. Coined from Greek and Latin roots, it is supposed to suggest "around the world." An utterly generic idea that really tells you nothing of interest about the company. But then, arguably, it doesn't matter. These are corporate names that customers hardly ever see. With Diageo for instance, we encounter only the brands it owns, like Guinness. The audience for these names are investors, who are supposedly much more interested in performance and the balance sheet. But they are still people. And they can still be engaged by a brand with an emotional appeal, or a good story, as Orange and Google have proved.

There was then a golden era for namers (if not necessarily for great names). In the late 1990s and early 2000s, the dot com boom took hold and branding agencies, and their naming practices in particular, made a mint. Firstly, there were loads of internet-based start-ups needing new names. It was also the height of the power of the brand, where it was often the starting point for a business rather than just a way to help you meet your commercial goals (and of course, the market supported this belief, as stocks soared in internet brands that hadn't ever made money, and didn't even seem to know how they would). Some of our clients at Interbrand weren't even very sure what the brands were going to *do* at all, once they existed. These were mere details that were going to get sorted out later. One venture capital firm got us to name at least three new brands in the space of about three weeks, none of which they could really explain, and none of which, as far as I can tell, ever did a day's business.

This culture had an effect on the names too. Provenance names – people and places – went out of fashion, as suddenly a sense of history seemed irrelevant to success. Instead, brands decided the internet had given them a new customer – younger, more laid back, wanting to see a brand as a mate rather than big stuffy thing to trust. As namers, we loved it. Anything was allowed. We named things Fatbrain and Kankan, while our competitors were coming up with SpeedyTomato and Leaping-Salmon. As you can see, the internet meant that, for a while, we abolished the space between words.

Another big feature of the internet boom in the late 1990s was the fact that anyone quick off the mark and hoping to make a quick buck or two could buy up "domain names" (words followed by .com, .net, .co.uk, or whatever) on the internet incredibly cheaply. Not surprisingly people got in there fast, buying up generic names like drugs.com or hotels.com, as well as those of plenty of well-known brands. This was a big naming problem, because domain names didn't work like trademark law. In the world of trademarks, products in different categories with the same name are allowed to coexist; think of Polo mints, the VW Polo, and Polo Ralph Lauren. This works on the basis that an average customer is not likely to confuse these products – you're not likely to walk into a newsagent's looking for something to sweeten your breath and walk out with a small hatchback car. But on the net, there is only one polo.com, so whoever got there first owned the most obvious domain name. In the early days, that wasn't even necessarily the people who owned the brands. Eventually the intellectual property laws were straightened out to give trademark owners effective first refusal on their own names, and the right to get back the ones that had been snapped up. Nevertheless, pretty soon most real words were taken as domain names – and the ones that weren't? Well you wouldn't really want to do business under those, to be honest.

The demand for domain names had two ramifications. Either companies spent megabucks to get hold of these real world domain names, sending a whole generation of cheeky, early-registering internet pups into wealthy early retirement. Or companies had to pay brand consultants like me to make up new words, for their businesses, that wouldn't already have been taken as dot coms.

It was the best of times; it was the worst of times. For a while we had tons of work, we had so many clients wanting a dot com (then as now, the default first choice when people are trying to guess what a brand's domain name might be) that we spent our entire lives coming up with extraordinarily weird names that, incredibly, had nevertheless already been registered by someone else. These were names that were so convoluted, so odd, and frankly so rubbish, that often we found ourselves sat in front of our computer screens in stupefaction that anyone else in the history of the universe had ever come up with that idea. However, two of my favourite names, WorldOnToast.com and FortyBlinks.com, were still free. Perhaps for obvious reasons, I LOVED them. My friend, brand guru Jeremy Faro, also came up with some of the most absurd names. Names, which like Jeremy, are so very Harvard. I present ShockingBeige and FinickyMagnet.

The WorldOnToast project ended up being called Peeled. com, before, inevitably, the superbrand behind the venture pulled the plug. I wonder if anyone's got them registered now? Go and check. They'll make you a fortune one day. Mark my words.

It meant that on every project we had to come up with thousands more names than before and then check if there was any possibility of any of them being free. It was frequently soul destroying watching a list of thousands of great names dwindle into four slightly below average ideas.

This climate was a significant factor in the explosion of names like Accenture and Altria which the press, particularly in the UK, found ridiculous and offensive, typically characterizing them as extravagant wastes of money. Often they were, but it was what you had to do at the time to get a usable name. Some companies saw a way round it by having a domain that was different to the actual brand name. The airline Go used go-fly, and a rival low cost airline used buzz-away. Neat idea, but it does complicate your communications, especially if you expect to do a lot of your business across the internet. It means whenever you promote your name, you need to promote a slightly different domain name at the same time.

The success of search engines, and Google in particular, was a big factor in killing that market dead (along with the disappearance of many of the internet speculators when times got hard). People realized they could rely on Google to find the websites they were after, even if they didn't know the domain name. They started typing "BBC" into Google before they attempted bbc.com, bbc.net, bbc.co.uk or wherever else they might guess they'd find the website they were looking for, because they felt that Google was usually the easiest way to do it. Suddenly the pressure was off companies to always find the most easily guessable website, and instead people concentrated on finding ways of getting the coveted "I'm feeling lucky" slot in their chosen area. A market disappeared. And my brand naming heyday was dead and buried.

As the internet exploded in the late 1990s, so did another type of naming. As Glyn Britton notes:

In the dot com era that gave us some great names like Yahoo! and Google, others were so seduced by the Internet that they forgot to name their company at all. In the real world nobody would ever think of calling their pet shop just "Pet Shop" and even if they did nobody in their right mind would then give them $120 million to market it. But that's what happened with Pets.com and a few other generically named dot coms.

It's ironic of course that these days we can't name many of the generic brands. Even in the net world order, brands, which build a reputation and emotional resonance for their customers, still seem to be more appealing than bland, generic ones.

Perhaps as a reaction to the awkward invented corporate names, the 1990s also saw a real trend for brand names based on really simple English names, many of which came out of branding agency Wolff Olins. They were behind names like Orange, Go, the credit card Goldfish, and Monday. Of course, this type of name has been around for a long time. Martin Lee says:

Penguin Books, Apple (record labels), Apple (computers), Virgin. All of these had no obvious connection to their product or industry but implied a type of spirit or daring which gave a hint of the values that drove the business. The fact that Penguin named their business in the 1920s gives them the edge, for me, over the others.

Wolff Olins brought this style of name to the forefront of naming. Some brands, like Orange, took the branding world by storm. Others, like Monday, had a more difficult birth. Monday was the new name for PricewaterhouseCoopers' consulting business, which was being separated from the rest of the company. The name Monday was part of a strategy to create the first real brand in the professional services market operating by the rules of consumer marketing. It followed the Wolff Olins design template we saw with Go – strong, simple typography with bold use of black, white, and bold highlight colours. It came loaded with attitude. And the idea behind the name was that this was the company that saw Mondays as an opportunity, the start of something, rather than the dreaded start of the working week and the end of the weekend. It was a bold idea, as you'd expect, but one that was typically derided by the press, and, it has to be said, by people in most businesses at the time. But, like Orange, I suspect that given time attitude would have done the trick. When the ridicule died down, it would have settled down into an interesting, distinctive brand.

But it never got that time. Just a few weeks into its short life, Monday went on permanent bank holiday. IBM bought the business, and pretty quickly rewrote history. It was as if Monday never existed. They simply said that they'd bought PwC Consulting, and pretty soon it was reborn for a second time as IBM Business Consulting Services (following IBM's model of making their main brand the hero, and simply naming their services descriptively).

The derision that Monday got highlights the strengths and weaknesses of this simple real word type of name. On the one hand, they can be quite appealing. As real words, they have strong associations – they're automatically more emotive, and seemingly more human than the Lucents and Agilents of the world. But the flipside of this is that they might just as well have the baggage of instinctive negative reactions, as Monday did. Lucent and Agilent don't; they just provoke mild distaste at their corporate blandness.

All this can be easy work as a namer, though. At Interbrand we used a freelance namer who did most of her work for Wolff Olins. No matter what brief we gave her, we got back a list of words any five year old looking around them could have come up with: Blue, Cloud, Blob, Field.

This sort of name has stayed popular in the world of marketing and the media, although they've become progressively weirder over the years. Look through magazines like Creative Review or Grafik and nearly every agency has one of these sort of names. I went to advertising agency WCRS in London the other day. As I walked into the building, I was confronted with a list of names of companies in the same group, presumably all advertising, marketing and media companies:

Dave
Meme
Personal
Element
Woo
Arena

You couldn't make it up.

A recent trend is for brands to use numbers as names. TV and radio channels and phone services have always done this, but it seems to be spreading. There's 3, the mobile phone brand owned by Hutchison Whampoa. And food group 3663 (named for the keys you'd touch on a phone if you were texting the word "food"). I'm actually on the board of an organization with a number as its brand – not-for-profit business writers' group, 26. We were named after the number of letters in the English Roman alphabet. After all, can you imagine trying to get a group of writers to agree on the right word to represent them?

Names like 3663 and 26 are nice because they encapsulate little stories in a neat way. Clearly, although there are a lot of numbers, not many of them are that memorable. However, the lower your number, the less distinctive it seems to be. 3 was named as a reference to the third generation mobile telephony technology it was spearheading, but was unfortunate to launch in the UK at almost exactly the same time as the new TV channel BBC3, using the song with the line, "Three, that's the magic number." People were confused as to which was which, and the problem has probably got worse as the other mobile phone brands have launched their 3G networks, and naturally been allowed to use the term itself, because it's the industry generic. Similarly, nearly every category of business has a brand trying to claim ownership of the number 1. In fact 1 is so generic that it usually has to be combined with something else to make it recognizable and distinctive – OneTel, The One Account and so on. Number naming is in vogue now, but I think the fad will be over pretty quick. As I write, discussions are going on about whether to allow single letter domains – things like a.com – to be registered. If it goes through, that will be the next naming trend, and they'll have just the same problems as with the numbers. If you like a bet, then put some money on that.

5

"why are you calling it that? Get a decent **answer** to that question"

The Fear

SO, WITH NEW NAMES FACING AN INEVITABLE storm of media ridicule, brands got "The Fear." Launching a new name seemed like a risky business, an easy way to open yourself up to the ridicule of the media and the opprobrium of your customers. Not surprisingly, brands went for the conservative option.

So, when Cadbury decided they wanted to add new chocolate bars to their portfolio, they didn't do it by developing new names and packaging, launched in a blaze of glory, as they had in the past. Before, they'd said here comes the Wispa, and done all the advertising and PR you'd expect. Or, a few years later, here comes Fuse, a product that leapt to the top of the chocolate charts but quickly fizzled like a primary school Catherine wheel.

No, this time, the new bars arrived wearing the name of an old favourite – Dairy Milk, one of the oldest chocolate brands going. So we got Dairy Milk with mint crisp, Dairy Milk with shortcake biscuit, Dairy Milk with orange pieces. The naming pattern was set: the name we know and love, plus a descriptor of the product. Don't frighten the horses. It also meant the death of a number of iconic brands, like Wispa and Cadbury's Caramel which morphed into mere siblings in this chocolate family: Dairy Milk bubbly, and Dairy Milk with caramel. Clearly, there's more going on here than just a naming problem. Cadbury were concertedly creating a super brand from one of their existing stars. But it is symptomatic of the time, which was characterized by the timidity of sticking to what you know rather than going out on a limb.

The great spur for the naming boom of the 1990s was commercial activity – corporations buying others, selling divisions, merging and demerging. And while much of this work tailed off in the first few years of the 21st century, some of it was still happening. Take Bass. A British brewer – in fact, owner of the first ever British trademark, the Bass red triangle – they'd grown by buying up pubs and hotels. And a few years later, they were splitting up again. The group sold their brewing arm – and so the Bass brand – to American giant Coors. That meant the corporate group needed a new name. They opted for the rather lofty Six Continents – since they operated outlets all over the world (although not, presumably, in Antarctica, the missing continent). Not surprisingly, it earned them a bit of ribbing from the British press, but not the critical onslaught others had suffered. Of course, being able to give a simple reason for the rebranding – that the sale of the brewing business meant they simply weren't allowed to use the Bass name any more – helped significantly. It's an example of how good PR can shape the reception of a new name. Nevertheless there was an odd mismatch between walking into a tiny English pub, and leaving with a receipt grandly announcing Six Continents Plc. It was definitely a name that hinted at the posh hotels end of their business.

Soon though, still in its first flash of corporate youth, Six Continents died a death. The two arms of the business – hotels and pubs – went their separate ways. The hotels half took their name from one of their most well-known chains, InterContinental (once again, straddling the globe in its ambitions). Which left the pubs group looking for a new name, one, which might feel a little more down to earth than its glitzy cousin, and one which wouldn't get them into media hot water. So this time, the group brought a name back from the dead: Mitchells & Butlers. They'd been part of the large number of businesses bought up by Bass on their way to the top. So here was a name from the company's past, quietly minding its own business, probably expecting to live out its days in some dusty file on some dusty shelf of a trademark lawyer's office.

But it fitted the bill perfectly. Firstly, it had a sense of provenance, a spirit that suited the idea of a group of British pubs – a fairly traditional business. And we've already seen that two names is code for "slightly higher quality than your average." The fact that these were two founders' names also gave the name that ring of truth, that smack of authenticity, which could put a stop to the media dogs foaming at the mouth. After all, what they really have a taste for is the whiff of consultancy smoke and mirrors. Not only did Mitchells & Butlers not need much explaining, but, of course, it didn't really take a gang of overpaid media types to think it up. So there was a nice story for the business pages too – a thrifty approach to running the business that might bode well for other areas too.

What the Dairy Milk brand extensions and the rebirth of Mitchells & Butlers have in common is that the names have a reason to exist. They are simple answers to the journalist's question, "So, why are you calling it that?" Get a decent answer to that question, and you'll save yourself a lot of trouble, not only with the media but with your own colleagues. I've seen people trying to explain away the lurking resonances of an abstract name we all know has been plucked at random from a list of also-rans that only just managed not to get shot down in flames by a trademark lawyer. Let me tell you, it's not a pretty sight. Whether the punters care at the end of the day, I'm not really sure. If they like what you do, and they can say your name, they're probably not that bothered. But it keeps the rest of us in rocket and sun-dried tomatoes.

These ideas all work because they present us with a story. You need a story to satisfy the human desire for explanation. The media pounced on names – like Accenture and Consignia – which seemed to have just come out of nowhere, and then totted up how much it had cost to come up with such nonsense. Which is why, I think, many of the most successful brands of recent times use names with a story behind them.

Take Google. Google was incorporated in 1998, and has quickly become a global mega brand, especially since its controversial IPO. And it has topped the poll, run by Interbrand's Brandchannel website, for the world's favourite brand (it seems to vie for the top spot every year with Apple, two brands who've made it their mission to humanize the scary world of technology. Perhaps that's why we're so gushingly grateful). So Google is young, as are its founders. Sergey Brin and Larry Page were computer science students at Stanford who stumbled on a way of getting little bits of information out of lots of stuff that's made them a fortune, and in its own way, changed the world. OK, maybe "stumbled" is a little unfair.

Where did the name come from? Well, a googol is in fact a real number; it's the name mathematicians give to the number ten followed by a hundred zeroes – it would take about a line and a half to write it for you, so I won't, just now, if you don't

> ## Egg
>
> British insurer Prudential wanted to launch a bank that was younger, funkier, and less stuffy than its competitors. It's another name the brand consultants love. Sophie Devonshire says:
>
> Whatever the name is, say it loud and say it proud. I love my Egg card even though the deal isn't as good as it was, partly because I adore the word egg and as a name think it works so well as a friendly place to put my nest-egg.
>
> Martin Lee says:
>
> The most you can hope for in naming a business for the first time is some kind of a signpost to the kind of business that you are. So, for instance, when financial services companies were all monolithic and intimidating, to call their business Egg gave them some genuine stand out and a point of difference. You immediately knew that you were getting a new approach to personal finance. If potential customers also happened to make connections such as "nest egg" that made them smile, then so much the better.

mind. It's a nerdy name for a nerdy idea. But remember that the initial audience for Google, and the people who were the springboard for its success, were computer nerds. Computer nerds who then went on to recommend it to their marginally less nerdy friends, until it reached technosimpletons like you and me (OK, you might be some kind of computer whizzkid, I don't know). So, for their audience, it was hitting the right kind of note – an in-joke that made the brand feel authentic to a key audience. But I think it's significant that they didn't just leave it as Googol, which is a funny looking arrangement of a word. That change to the end of the word, -ol to -le, makes all the difference. Firstly, it makes it look like a normal English word. Not one that does exist (or did, then), but one which could. It looks familiar, and even sounds quite fun. Perhaps it's the "o" and the repetition of the "g"s that you find in words like oodle, caboodle, giggle, even googoo.

It's not a cold, technological-sounding, made up name at all, but is altogether more human, and is reinforced by the way the logo looks: multi-coloured, mainly lower case, exactly the sort of thing you might find in a children's storybook. Just what you'd expect of a company that has "don't be evil" as its internal mantra.

Starbucks is another brand, and another name that has taken the world by storm. And it's not the name of anyone to do with the business. So it sort of sits there, unexplained, but definitely linguistically Anglo-Saxon, and even, consciously or not, with a couple of American associations: the stars and stripes, and the big bucks it wanted to make. Actually, this might be a classic case of reading more into the name than is really there. Starbuck is a character in *Moby-Dick* (a book the founders loved – so much so that the chain was nearly called the slightly unsavoury *Pequod*, after the boat). Of course, most customers, and probably most Starbucks staff, will never know. But it doesn't matter. All that matters is that there *is* a story there, if you want to look for one. It's a fairly run of the mill name in the first place, but it has some kind of a reason to exist.

I think this little trend will go on for a while yet. The marketing world is currently obsessed with the idea of authenticity – products and experiences which feel more wholesome, genuine, unspun, altogether more real than those offered by the superbrands of the late 20th century. The rise of authenticity has been used to explain the rise of such diverse phenomena as book groups and farmers' markets. Names with stories behind them are an expression of this trend, too. They say there's something real here, something to find out, you're not being conned, or marketed to. So I think that should be the test of the new great names: how good is your answer to, "Why's it called that, then?"

6

"I love the name **Half Man, Half Biscuit**, but who remembers them now?"

You'll never walk alone

ONE OF THE BIG REASONS WHY NAMING PROCESSES GO wrong is that people's expectations of them are wrong. They're looking for the perfect name, the name that brilliantly encapsulates everything they want to say about their new brand, and is available as a trademark, and as a dot com, and doesn't mean "manure" in Polish.

Well, the bad news is that that name doesn't exist. Never look for the perfect name. Even the good ones only become perfect with 20/20 hindsight. And a good name can't succeed if the product is lousy. When I asked Martin Lee of Acacia Avenue what made a good brand name, he said:

Facetiously, I'd say it was having a good business. There's nothing intrinsically good about, say, Cadbury or certainly Tesco or Asda, but the businesses that sit behind those names are excellent. You might have a fantastic name for a business but if it's a useless business, so what? It's a bit like bands. I love the name Half Man, Half Biscuit but who remembers them now? U2 is a pretentious, silly name for a band, but they are the most famous band on the planet.

Assuming the product isn't just plain lousy, the problem is usually that people want the name to communicate too much. After all, most names are just a few letters long, a few words at most. If you could say everything in that amount of room, why would you ever write a brief, or a mission statement, or website? Your name would just be able to do it all itself.

Of course, that doesn't happen. So you're not looking for that. You're looking for a name which does part of the job – communicates some of the things you want to communicate – and makes it easy to do the rest. And how do you do the rest? Well, you've got lots to work with. There are three main ones: a strapline, design, and advertising, though PR is becoming increasingly relevant. Which of these you use probably depends on how much money you've got to spend to explain your name.

How does it work? Well, you need to look at which things your name *is* communicating, then which it's not, and compensate for them. So a name like British Airways is entirely descriptive. It tells you what business the company is in, and where they are based. Nothing more than that, really. You might guess that they might try to exploit a sense of "Britishness" in the way they serve their customers, but you'd only be surmising that from the name. With a name so practical, down to earth, and logical, they needed to find a way to inject some warmth and emotion into our perception of that brand. So for many years they used a strapline alongside the name, "The world's favourite airline." The word "favourite" takes us into territory that is much warmer and fuzzier.

And then think of the reverse. When British Airways launched their new low-cost brand they called it Go. Full of energy and enthusiasm. A positive, emotional name. But for a new brand, it really didn't explain what they did, or give them any of the kind of credibility you might want from someone who is asking you to step into a metal tube they intend to take into the sky. So they chose a strapline that was descriptive and factual; everything the name wasn't, "The low cost airline from British Airways." In both of these cases, BA are making sure they have both functional and emotional messages covered, but through different combinations of name alongside strapline.

A few years ago, the British charity The Spastics Society had a problem. Their very name included a word that had for many years been used, not least in school playgrounds, as a deroga-tory term for people with all sorts of physical disabilities, but particularly cerebral palsy – which is the disability the word "spastic" originally described. The name of the charity had in fact become offensive to its own members. So they decided to change it, and to be quite brave about it. They chose the name Scope. It was a bold move; a category-breaker, in fact. It was one of the first charity names to suggest the positive benefits of their work, rather than the group of people they worked with (like the Children's Society) or the problem they were trying to alleviate (like the League Against Cruel Sports). But The Spastics Society had been a household name, with charity shops on high streets up and down the land, so they needed to make sure people still knew who they were, or at least where the focus of their work was. After all, giving people "scope" is the aim of many different charities and organizations. So when the new name was introduced, they also used a descriptive strapline alongside it, "For people with cerebral palsy." In recent years, they've changed the descriptor, "About cerebral palsy." They also added another line to emphasize their mission, "For equality for disabled people." Both lines do things the name can't. Another dynamic duo.

But you don't just have straplines to help. The beauty of a brand name is that it's usually seen in a context that the brand owner can control visually – as a logo, website, ad, letter, and so on. That means you can use the way the name is presented to emphasize or counterbalance elements of the name. The example I've always loved here is Orange, the mobile phone network founded by Hutchison Whampoa but now owned by France Télécom. They launched first of all in the UK, with a brief to make a big dent in the fortunes of the two established players in the market – BT Cellnet (then owned by British Telecom, but then demerged as O_2 and now bought by Telefónica) and Vodafone. Both were being targeted primarily at business customers, with very cold, technical sounding names. Orange's first job was just to sound different. Choosing a colour with no associations to the product whatsoever was a brave move. But that sort of a name does allow you to form different sorts of associations, as well as more emotional associations, and that's exactly what Orange did. A bold and clever name, it sounded not only unusual and different, but also more human and easier to relate to.

Of course, it's not just the name. The way the Orange visual identity is used shapes how we think of the brand. Hutchison could have treated Orange as a very fun name. You can see it now – blobby type, fruit as a logo, heck, maybe it would even shoot water at you. But in a time when mobile phones were still a novelty, and still something slightly mystifying to most of us, would you have trusted a brand like that to deliver you a piece of technical kit that was reliable, and apparently sophisticated? Maybe not. So Orange made clever move number two. The visual identity is very confident and "professional" – three colours only: black, white, and an incredibly vivid orange. The type is clean and classic. The lines of the identity are sleek and square. So the Orange brand actually gives you a rather subtle message. From its name you get friendliness and distinctiveness, and from its visuals you get calm and technological nous. The result is a brand that feels accessible but credible, human but somehow visionary at the same time.

But the combination of messages doesn't end with Orange's name and logo. There's a strapline too, which synthesizes the quite complex signals they've been communicating into a great, classic line, "The future's bright, the future's Orange." When they launched the brand, they made bold use of simple, everyday words, which set them a world apart from the aloof and technocratic language of their competitors; posters simply said "hello" in the Orange orange on black. But what most commentators tend to forget now is that Orange's launch advertising also featured another sort of message that was lacking in both the name and the rest of the branding work. Unlike the other mobile phone networks, if you went to Orange, your calls would be billed by the second, rather than being rounded up to the nearest minute. Orange didn't talk about being low cost, or cheap – that wouldn't have fitted with the sophistication of the rest of their identity – but they did make a big deal about this very functional message – per second billing – one that was much more about a logical calculation of value rather than the fluffy stuff about brands. But alongside the fluffy stuff about brands, it made a killer combination. And despite a slightly baffled reaction from the industry media when the new brand was launched (and was called Orange of all things. Crazy!) and despite being third mover in the sort of sector where being first usually counts for most, Orange won legions of customers – fans even – and even made it to the number one place in the UK mobile phone market. But the name would never have done it on its own.

The period in which you launch a name on the outside world can be crucial. In fact, that's true of all branding work. One of the most famous branding disasters of recent years was the project which has become known as the British Airways tailfins. The airline had long been seen as very British, with all the positive and negative associations that come wrapped up, part and parcel, with the UK brand itself: polite, but a bit stuffy. BA wanted to move the perceptions of their brand away from pure Britishness into something slightly more modern, and more universal. They shied away from changing the name, though they did, naturally, think of shortening it just to the initials BA. But with that feeling like a step too far, they decided on changing their look to reflect the idea of being a "citizen of the world." Their design agency came up with a really bold answer to that brief. Instead of a standard tailfin, the same on every plane (which was then a stylized version of the Union flag), they proposed something more radical. Each plane would have a different tailfin, based on a piece of native art from one of the countries BA flew to. It was a brave idea (and a lucky one for the woman who got the very jammy brief of travelling the world buying up art to stick on the back of the planes).

British Airways spent a lot on their new look, and launched it in spectacular fashion. But they launched it in a time of PR strife: their poor industrial relations were making headlines in every British newspaper, and the media presented the rebrand as a spectacular waste of money, a case of priorities truly in the wrong place. Naturally, the right-wing press sought to present the rebrand as a rejection, by one of the country's biggest, most influential companies, of Britishness. A final nail in the coffin came when Margaret Thatcher, the ex-prime minister, but still an influential icon to the *Daily Telegraph*-reading passengers of BA, covered up the tailfin on a model BA plane with her handkerchief to express her dissatisfaction at the move. The airline had been well and truly hankied, if not handbagged.

Faced with a backlash, BA wobbled. Despite a warm reception for the design work elsewhere in the world, the British reaction scared them on to the defensive. The British media – with their canine nose for fear – pounced on BA's insecurity and their slightly lacklustre attempts to persuade the public of the logic behind the move. Soon British Airways were making commitments to repaint the tailfins, back to a version of the Union flag, at yet another spectacular cost.

The work has since often been hailed as a design classic, but not surprisingly as a commercial disaster. The suspicion remains that had BA had the courage of their convictions, really standing firm in their belief in the logic behind the truly unique, original design job, there would still be Chinese calligraphy and Dutch china patterns flying round at 30,000 feet today. But with the PR wobble, the branding was done for.

The same seems to apply to names. The launch of a name demands an unshakeable confidence in the rightness and brilliance of the name you've chosen. And you need to be able to explain your decision. Otherwise, there's always the danger of doing a Consignia.

As we've seen, Consignia was announced as the new name for the holding company for the UK's post offices in 1991, to immediate uproar from the typically scandal-hungry British media. Why did the Post Office need a new name? Were we going to have to say that we were going to post a letter at the Consignia? Would the friendly chap delivering letters from loved ones of a morning have to be known as the Consigniaman?

The answer to all these questions was no. Consignia was only ever going to be the name of the holding company. They were expanding into Europe, and had been lumbered with the typical problems of a descriptive name – after all, the British Post Office was just one of many European post offices. So they needed to be able to register something unique to act as an umbrella. It's not a great name. But it was certainly no worse than many of the bland neologisms that appeared around that time, and more importantly, it wasn't a name the general public was ever going to see. The high street Post Office was still going to be the Post Office. Only the company behind it would be different.

But Consignia did an appalling job of explaining that, leaving some poor old chap from the design agency that came up with the name desperately trying to explain the strategy. Meanwhile, postmen were interviewed on the news, not having been told about the change and whipped up into a frenzy about how much the whole rebranding had cost, dismissing the whole thing as utterly absurd. Not surprisingly, a few months later, Consignia was quietly ditched and renamed (again!) Royal Mail Group.

But compare this experience with Centrica, another typically anonymous corporate name. This was the new name for the holding company behind British Gas, another venerable British industry which had been privatized. They wanted to expand beyond energy into credit cards, and even bought the AA, Britain's leading roadside recovery service. Understandably, British Gas started to look like an odd name for a company with all of those interests. And again, the public-facing brand of British Gas wasn't changing; there was just a new name for the city analysts in the know. But Centrica explained better what was happening and stuck to their guns (and this was also before the British press really got their claws into us evil branding consultants) and no one batted an eyelid. A decent PR campaign, and Centrica and British Gas are still going strong nine years later. And it goes to show it's really not just the name. What you do with it can make or break the brand.

7

"the main rule is that **many** heads are better than one"

Into the playpen

SO, WE'VE THOUGHT ABOUT OUR STRATEGY AND DEFINED a naming brief. We've got realistic expectations. And we know what we'll have to do when we've got the name. Now all we have to do is get it.

People always ask how namers come up with names. And not surprisingly, they always seem slightly disappointed with the answer, "Er, we just sort of write them down on a list on a piece of paper." It seems that somehow that's too easy. Or too straight. Some clients are clearly sitting there hoping for the answer, "Oh, we do it in cocaine-fuelled brainstorms at the Groucho Club." But that's a million miles from the truth.

Most of the legwork in agencies is done by people sitting there with a pen and paper, writing lists. There are some terribly modern types who just type it into a computer, but I find it's the doodling that really helps you come up with names. It is quite exciting to take a name like Ocado, which has ended up on carrier bags, websites, adverts on buses, and best of all, vans (that actually drive past my front door) and go back and find the piece of paper on which you first wrote it down. Because of the very fast churn of naming projects, and the really long lead-time with most brands between naming them and their actual eventual appearance in the real world, going back to the original names feels a bit like archaeology. They become like artefacts, Rosetta stones or cave paintings. Actually my similes here are really to hide the fact that when a name gets launched, everyone on a naming team scuttles back to their notes to see who came up with it. It's like the Oxford English Dictionary. You're looking for the first attested use of each word. There are annoying projects where everyone has come up with the same idea, and it's impossible to prove who came up with it first. There's nothing worse than having to take the credit as a team, rather than the unalloyed joy of basking in the glory of your own personal creative genius.

The main rule with naming is that many heads are better than one. You've got more chance of hitting the winners if you take an hour of eight people's brains rather than eight hours of one person's. The best thing to do is to get thousands of people to help you, and that's what some companies do. They run competitions to name their new brands. It might be as easy as setting up an e-mail address and getting people to send in their ideas. Throw in a bottle of champagne (oh, and the unalloyed joy of basking in the glory of your own personal creative genius) and watch the names roll in. This does take someone with a modicum of creative nous at the end of the e-mail address to rifle through the replies. Usually the first couple of hundred people write in and say, "Hey guys, couldn't we call it Focus?" before reeling off a two paragraph rationale for why they've come up with what in fact is the most obvious name in the world. For almost any brief! The recipient of all this needs to spot the wheat lying among the chaff. Indeed, a canny idea is to do this sort of thing alongside a naming process with some "proper" namers. Then whatever happens always, always, always tell people that the winning name came out of the competition. It gives people a nice little sense of internal corporate pride, and the press loves it. You will be lauded for your pragmatism and thriftiness at a time when other companies are squandering thousands on jumped-up oiks like me.

On the other hand, you could do what this person did on the Business Bricks website, spotted by brand consultant Sophie Devonshire. Just ask other people to do it for you. It's a good illustration of how subjective it all is (everyone thinks their idea is brilliant) and how obvious the first set of ideas usually is:

Name Charlie's business

Matt Weston, 29 Sep | Comments (25)
Here today: NAME CHARLIE'S BUSINESS
"We (Standard Office Cleaning) need a new name. The word standard nowadays means boring and average – and we're anything but. We're growing rapidly and, whereas most cleaning companies pay low-skilled employees a low-wage, we reward our workforce with a capital stake in each individual contract."
CHARLIE MOWAT
Can you help Charlie? Comments are open.
And winner gets a bottle of champagne.

Reader comments

25 comments so far:

Stuart Whitman says:

How about Acclaim Cleaners – takes your philosophy of rewarding employees but also shows clients what kind of cleaning company you are.
By Stuart Whitman on 29 Sep

Glenda Shawley says:

Sounds a great business. A first thought (others might come later) how about "Top of the Mops"?
By Glenda Shawley on 29 Sep

Mark Evamy says:

Shiny Happy People...?
By Mark Evamy on 29 Sep

Lesley Kershaw says:

How about Fresh Concept as the name as well as the approach.
By Lesley Kershaw on 29 Sep

Charlie Mowat says:

Some nice ideas there. "Top of the Mops" made me laugh (which might not be a good thing if it makes potential clients laugh...). Looking forward to seeing some more.
By Charlie Mowat on 29 Sep

Ian Edwards says:

Two suggestions – Spruce! or Spring Cleaners (two easy logos here).
By Ian Edwards on 29 Sep

Mel Wilby says:

How about "Charlie's Angels?" Anyone who cleans my office is a real angel if they do it right.
By Mel Wilby on 29 Sep

Tom Moir says:

"Marks and Spotless."
By Tom Moir on 29 Sep

Malcolm Swallow says:

1. Non-Standard Office Cleaning 2. Top2Bottom.
By Malcolm Swallow on 29 Sep

Kamal Thapen says:

Name at present seems to imply a basic cleaning service. How about "Care Office Cleaning" but only if you specialize in offices; otherwise drop the office.
By Kamal Thapen on 29 Sep

Kim Dellanzo says:

How about 1. M.O.P.S. Motivated, Outstanding, People, Shining ... 2. Unsung Heroes 3. Everyday Magic.
By Kim Dellanzo on 29 Sep

Ewan Makepeace says:

Spick and Span.
Squeaky Clean.
By Ewan Makepeace on 30 Sep

Paul McCormick says:

TCS – Total Cleaning Solutions.
By Paul McCormick on 30 Sep

Toby Wallis says:

"Squeaky." Says clean, says fun, will stick in the mind.
By Toby Wallis on 30 Sep

Julia Stebbing says:

I suggest Gleam Team or Office Gleam Team.
By Julia Stebbing on 30 Sep

Dan Rice says:

OSS – Office Sortation Squad.
Complete Clean Team.
Spick n Span.
CCC – Charlie's Cleaning Crew (maybe not then).
By Dan Rice on 30 Sep

Lyn Dean says:

I think some of these suggestions are brilliant. I just wished I had asked the same question when I started my little business. I love

Top Of The Mops. I think it's nice if your customers laugh and find it funny, because they are more likely to remember it. Also Shiny Happy People – everyone will remember the song and then your business. I just wish I could think of something that good.
By Lyn Dean on 1 Oct

Alan Crockford says:

I'll second Squeaky. Also good if you move into pest control. "We're Squeaky – so they're not."
By Alan Crockford on 2 Oct

John Wright says:

Just had a nosy at your website and names to date. Without further waffle...Integrated Cleaning Services.
By John Wright on 3 Oct

Wallace says:

"Spotless precision" (motto = the way to ensure you always keep your office clean).
By Wallace on 3 Oct

Jemima House says:

Fresh solutions. I was going to use this for another arm of our contract cleaning business – cleaning chemicals hence the solution pun – but I'm not using it now so u can have it – plus I love champagne...
By Jemima House on 4 Oct

Alex Smith says:

I like Squeaky too. I think some of the others, like Top of the Mops, are funny and quirky but probably not right. Something that implies that you will take on the horrible stuff, which your clients might not want to do. Remember one of Matt Bricks' last year about Mr Muscle – "Loves the jobs you hate." So, perhaps, Easy Office Cleaning or Direct Office Cleaning. I also quite like Top2Bottom but I wonder how long text-speak will last.
By Alex Smith on 5 Oct

Leigh Garland says:

High Standard Office Cleaning? Or how about POLISH or SHINE?
Erm ... CharPeople (think Char ladies, but Charlies people ...
hmm ...). Oooh, I know, how about ... SHINE – we wipe the floor
with anyone else!
By Leigh Garland on 5 Oct

Charlie Mowat says:

A big thank you to everyone for their ideas. I'll let you know
what we settle on ...
By Charlie Mowat on 9 Oct

Charlie Mowat says:

All. We eventually settled on The Clean Space Partnership. The
partnership word aiming to communicate how we operate. What
do you think?
By Charlie Mowat on 25 Oct

Well! Total Cleaning Solutions (oh dear) and more bloody
initials to Top of the Mops. That's pretty much the entire naming
spectrum covered just there. See how people automatically start
adding straplines to give the name more resonance.

So, because many hands make light work, a natural way to
do naming is in a brainstorm. Glyn Britton says:

The hard bit of naming is the creative process, especially when
the brief is very tight. The best namers I've worked with, as
well as having an aptitude for words, are brilliant at running
brainstorms that really encourage lateral thinking.

But the naming brainstorm is a funny old beast. Most people
try them before they call for the branding reinforcements, but
run them really badly and have to ring up a namer about five
minutes before the brand is due to launch. So, in danger of
writing myself out of a job, I'm going to tell you how I run

them. It's not the only way, and I'm not claiming it's the best way (although naturally I secretly think it is) but it works. At this point I must stress my undying and eternal devotion to the utterly brilliant and utterly inimitable Josephine Seccombe. Josephine is a professional facilitator. She was also a trainer we used at Interbrand in London to help people like me run workshops, and things like naming brainstorms. Josephine's brainstorms were so much better than the haphazard and lacklustre excuses for brainstorms we conducted before that I have since nicked the vast majority of her techniques, passed them off as my own and watched new colleagues gaze at my apparent charisma and professionalism. But I could never run one with anything like Josephine's strict and steely generosity. So for the following section, thank her, not me.

1. Have 6 people or more

Less than six and it somehow feels a bit limp and wishy washy. You need to get a bit of momentum going, a bit of energy in the room (sorry, I come over a bit new age guru when I'm put in charge of a group of people). In fact, you can have a lot of people in a naming group. Up to 15 or 20, if you can manage them – i.e. stop them talking over you, or gossiping in small groups. And, really importantly, the person in charge of the brainstorm shouldn't be trying to come up with names, even if the subject is their baby, literally or figuratively. Otherwise their mind wanders into trying to think up great ideas, and off running the group. It's the facilitator's job to keep the thing rolling and to make sure that everyone's having a super time.

2. Start with a brief

I think you get the most out of a brainstorm when you give people all the functional information at the beginning. What's the name for? Where will it appear? What countries are you going to use the name in? All that kind of stuff. Getting this clear at the start means that people are usually coming up with things that are roughly in the right sort of area. The shorter the brief, the better.

3. Don't go on

I tend to do naming brainstorms in about an hour, or if I'm feeling really confident about how interesting a brief is, an hour and half. Much more than that and most people's concentration span has gone, and if you're the facilitator you then have to work incredibly hard to keep doing new things to hold people's attention. It's like being a primary school teacher, in fact. And who'd want to do that?

4. Horseshoe, no table

OK, this is me getting really pernickety now and playing the facilitator as prima donna. I don't like a big table in the middle of a room where I'm brainstorming. Firstly, it makes it feel just like another boring old meeting, so it's harder to get people to think a bit more laterally than they normally do, which is what you really need for naming. And secondly, it definitely acts as a barrier. People hide behind it. Somehow, the table makes people feel secure about not saying their ideas out loud. What you want is to get a bit of a team dynamic going, where everyone can see each other and they're all building on each other's ideas. I think this works best when you set up a horseshoe of chairs around the facilitator and his or her accoutrements (in my case, usually just a trusty old flipchart).

5. Don't let them say anything

Now we're getting serious. This is really important, and this is where most naming brainstorms go wrong. Of course, I don't mean your participants shouldn't speak at all. That would be a terrible brainstorm. But I have a rule that says you should express every idea as a name. They shouldn't speak except to come up with something that really could be the name – something they could see on a website, on a business card, on the bottle, or wherever it's really going to appear. This gives the session real focus. I think it's crucial because otherwise the conversation goes round and round the houses without ever getting to any actual ideas. For example, people often say that we need some names that really suggest "freshness." But then they think they've done their bit by suggesting something, and then don't come up with any names. I tell them that if they want the group to come up with names about freshness, then they should just come up with one, shout it out, and if the idea works, the group will understand what that person's doing and build on it. For the same reason, I don't let people explain where their ideas have come from, or question other people about theirs. If it's good enough, we'll get it.

You have to be pretty tough to really enforce this, especially if you're a young facilitator trying to tell a 65-year-old chief executive to stop telling everyone else what to do, and have some ideas himself. This is the other agenda of the constant interjector. Sometimes they are trying to cover up their own lack (or perceived lack) of creativity. But more often they are trying covertly to direct the session the way they want it to go. Fair enough, you might think, if it's their project and their money that's paying you to be there. But it makes for a very unhealthy atmosphere in a brainstorm; the participants feel it's a charade where one person is secretly in charge, and you as the facilitator feel like a puppet. You need to straighten these things out before the session. What everyone's role is, what the "project owner" wants out of the brainstorm, and an understanding that it will go where the facilitator wants it to go. You may need to flirt with being thought of as a dictator, but it really, really pays dividends.

6. Write EVERY name down

The other reason why brainstorms fail is that they're often too judgmental. Someone comes up with an idea, someone else looks for all the potential problems with it (which is particularly easy to do with a name), or worse ridicules it, and slowly but surely the whole thing ends up juddering to a creaking, painful halt. Why would you come up with an idea if you think everyone is just going to tear it to pieces? What most brainstorms are left with at the end of an hour is about five names, which have been discussed – or rather, criticized – to death, leaving nothing that anyone really likes, and an air of quiet desolation hanging over your exciting new brand. That's when people call in the consultants.

So instead, my brainstorms always have two parts, which you need to explain right at the start of the session. In the first, the group comes up with names. They just shout them out, and the facilitator writes them all down. There is no evaluation at all – positive or negative. I don't even let people say, "That's a great idea, I love it!" Again, saying that seems harsh, but it implies the other ideas aren't great, which will intimidate some people into not speaking. Once you tell people they're not allowed to evaluate as we go along, you'll see some people trying to do it through their body language, or little noises that aren't quite words. I ruthlessly stamp on that, too. It's important that the facilitator writes down everything – including ideas that people suggest as jokes – otherwise it gives the impression that the facilitator is evaluating, by editing the ideas. And in any case, a really good idea might come out of something that starts off as a joke.

This process ends up being much closer to the way the namer works, spewing out loads and loads of ideas rather than agonizing over a handful. It makes for a much more productive session; it's naming as a numbers game. You'll probably end up with hundreds of names, most of which won't work, or are just plain terrible. But it's still a faster route to more genuinely interesting ideas than the way most brainstorms get done. Another tip is to number each idea as it comes out, always writing down the next number in the sequence as soon as you've written down the name that someone's come up with. It sets up the expectation that the ideas are going to keep on coming. Because I'm a words person, and not really a numbers one, I often get very confused with my numbering in the heat of the brainstorm. That doesn't matter one bit. How many you come up with isn't the point, but the expectation is.

How do you get people coming up with names? Well, lots of different ways. And, in fact, you need to run a naming session in lots of different small chunks because people's brains work so differently. Exercises that some people find easy will be a nightmare for others, and vice versa. Some people are very visual, some very verbal, others more "kinesthetic" (give them a piece of Plasticene to play with while they're thinking. It keeps

> ## Rocket
>
> Rocket is one of those names that I wish I'd thought of, every time I see it. They are a British retailer which sells "meal packs." Usually in commuter train stations, they provide you with a pack of ingredients ready prepared for you to throw together when you get home. I think it's designed to make young professionals feel they're being good and really cooking, rather than just heating up a ready meal.
>
> Rocket is the perfect name. Of course, it suggests speed. It tells you this is somewhere you'll be able to quickly buy something and quickly prepare. But when Rocket appeared on the market, the leaf rocket (or roquette, or arugula if you're American) was the recherché item on British restaurant menus (so sophisticated you see, I even have to use French vocabulary). Along with pine nuts and sundried tomatoes, rocket is exactly the kind of slightly posh ingredient their market aspired to buy. And of course, it gave you an image of something fresh and green, which was just right for the product. In fact, it would have been a great name for Ocado (of which more later).
>
> It was a name that worked on a number of levels, yet still seemed really simple and accessible. But it seems the product was less successful. Rocket has disappeared from many of its sites, seemingly struggling to succeed (like its competitor LeapingSalmon). It just goes to show a great name won't rescue a product that the public doesn't want.

them happy). Typically, you want a brainstorm to start with the really obvious stuff, while people are warming up. Then open up a bit into things that are more unlikely – things they'd probably never have come up with under their own steam. Finally, as they're getting a little bit tired, funnel all the ideas back down into something safer. If you've got a long time to fill then you can use this pattern several times over, constantly opening up and closing down the brief.

The best way to get the obvious stuff out is just with a brain dump: asking people to express all the ideas that have been going round their heads before the brainstorm. People might say they haven't got any, but if people know what the brainstorm is going to be about then that's really, really unlikely. They're just shy. A quite brutal way to get over people's natural inhibitions is to start by getting each person to say a name. That way, everyone has participated, right from the off, and they've all got over the most embarrassing hurdle. Otherwise some people would sit there for an hour and not say anything, if you let them. The brain dump also increases your chances of flushing out people's secret weapons early. Some people are pretty scared by the thought of coming up with names on the spot, so they do lots of preparation beforehand, coming up with names they can pepper through the session. I'd rather have those out at the beginning of the session, so for the rest of it people are all in the same boat, all engaged, and all trying to be spontaneously creative. It's not a competition, unless everyone in the room is a professional namer, in which case it really is, each vying for the glory of saying the killer name out loud. People also have often got a "favourite" name that they've come up with (or maybe just discussed) before the session. Again, if it's out early, it stops it being deployed at an important moment and effectively manipulating the session.

Next I try something a little more taxing, but not too scary. Some kind of visualization for example. It works like this. Take an aspect of the brief that you can translate into a personal emotion or sensation – usually things like power, satisfaction, teamwork, freshness … the usual brand suspects. Get the participants to get really comfortable in their seats, and to close their eyes. Then present them with a scenario that's the opposite of that sensation – a scenario where they feel impotent, dissatisfied, isolated, or dirty. Really ham it up. Make them feel it physically. Make them hate that feeling. And then, tell them you're going to take that feeling away (this is where you start feeling powerful, like some superhuman hypnotherapist mega hero). At a certain point, you'll clap, or snap your fingers, or shout, and you'll tell them to feel the opposite. What's important is that the opposite scenario is presented much more vaguely than the first one. That's because you want them to imagine it – to see it in whatever way comes to them instinctively (because these are the associations you want them to milk in coming up with names for you). Get them to imagine the scenario in sensual terms – what it looks like, tastes like, sounds like, feels like, smells like, even. Then with their eyes still closed, get them to come up with names that sum up that sensation. Maybe they'll even imagine the name is actually the name for the place they've come up with in their heads. They probably won't just have one name; they'll make several attempts to find the name for the sensation they're feeling, or build on ideas of the others. If you're lucky, the more adventurous ones among them will even start to make up names that sum up that feeling – joining existing words together, blending them, or inventing them from scratch.

They should be starting to loosen up now linguistically. They've also just done something very solitary, so it makes sense to get them to do something a little more sociable, just by way of contrast. Hopefully they're feeling a little brave. So now it's time to push them, maybe even scare them a little. We need them to completely lose their inhibitions. I normally put them in pairs at this point, and tell them they're in a train carriage. I get them to imagine they're having one of those embarrassing train carriage conversations, where the other person starts talking, and you end up having to make polite chit-chat about where they're heading, the weather, their jobs, all the usual small talk malarkey (maybe these sort of conversations are only so mortifyingly embarrassing if you're British). And then just as I'm about to get them to start talking to one another, I tell them they're going to be doing this in a language they're making up. You will rarely see such a look of abject terror come so consistently across the faces of an entire roomful of people. In a few, this look of terror will break into acutely embarrassed peals of laughter. For some, to be honest, during the rest of the exercise, the look of terror never really goes away.

So they will start their conversations ever so tentatively, wishing a little bit that they were dead. The sneaky ones will try to use a second language that they actually know, saving them a tiny bit of embarrassment. Obviously you as the facilitator are unlikely to know every language that they could be talking, but if it sounds too fluent right from the off, they're probably up to mischief. What most produce starts off like baby talk, but as they get into it, it'll get more complex and more sophisticated. So now you need to up the level of the energy in the room, so that they get really expressive with their new language. Get them to talk to their partner (still in the language they're making up, of course) about something they're really passionate about. Weirdly, this makes them actually *want* to speak, despite the fact they're having to use this odd new tongue. Get them to try to persuade the other person to do something. You'll find that what started off as two separate languages in each pair starts to mutate into a common language (or a lingua franca, at least).

At this point, when the room is loud, lively, and full of energy, introduce the naming brief, or one aspect of it. Get them to talk about this great new product, service or company (or whatever the brand is). Get them to communicate its features and benefits in their new language. Hopefully some of them now are starting to enjoy it a little. All in all you can keep this going for about a couple of minutes before they start to remember they are doing something truly, truly ridiculous.

What it does do for you, which is useful for the rest of the brainstorm, is get over the problem that lots of people have when they come to naming for the first time, which is inventing new words. It's just quite an odd thing to do, and probably most of us haven't had to do it since we were at school, naming strange lands or characters in our stories (actually, I've done that in workshops – seeing the brand as those lands and characters, and letting yourself regress to your nine year old self to name it). But lots of great brand names depend on people having the gumption to do it – Coca-Cola, Kodak, Tesco and the like. The made up language exercise forces people to do it, and after that, they're usually much less reticent. Having said that, I must give you a bit of a warning that there are some people who are just too self-conscious to cope with that exercise. They just clam up, and will probably never be the sort of person who comes up with invented names. Fingers crossed, though, it will give most people a bit of confidence that they can do it, which will help during the rest of the session. In fact, it even helps if you're not trying to create those kinds of names, because once you've done it, everything else feels like a doddle. So, when people are back to being just themselves, I ask them what the name for the brand was in their invented language, and to keep coming up with alternatives that convey a similar spirit.

What else have I done? I've used music to create particular moods; I've got people to draw random pictures and see how it inspires them; I've got people to close their eyes and touch things, smell things or taste things which might trigger the right mood (although Josephine's top tip here is never to get people to taste ice cream, if they're naming ice cream. People's imagination of an experience is always more exciting than the reality). Some people respond well to constraints – giving them a particular letter to start all their names with, so at least they have somewhere to begin. I've used lists of metaphors: if this brand were a colour, what would it be? Which place? What time of day? You can try anything that gets people's brains thinking a little laterally.

My dream scenario is that the brainstorm starts to "tick over" like the engine of a car, just idling in a tree-lined driveway. Brainstorms often start off very speedily, with ideas coming out thick and fast. Apart from anything else, it's incredibly difficult being the facilitator, trying to remember all the names people have shouted out in the last minute and writing them down. But also, that sort of a breakneck pace isn't sustainable. Your participants will tire themselves out. My ideal is that the brainstorm slows down a bit, but that ideas come out nice and steadily (think of it like the sustainable development of the creative world, rather than slash and burn). Sometimes this can go on for ten minutes or so, each person's ideas building on the others', giving me plenty of time to write them down. When it's working best, I don't have to do anything. The group becomes self-running, without me having to feed them any kind of stimulation. It's a lovely feeling. Of course, it makes the facilitator's job look incredibly easy. My mum came to one of my naming brainstorms once for a coffee product (seeing as she almost single-handedly kept the British coffee industry going throughout the 1980s). Obviously, highly irregular, since I was giving the £30 we paid punters to come to the "creative consumer groups" (all assiduously claimed back from the client, on top of our fees, of course) back to my family, but what can I tell you? Anyway, the workshop went well, and I managed to avoid being too weirded out by having my mum sitting there. But on the way out, she said, "I think I could do your job. It's quite easy, really, isn't it?" I explained my principle of the brainstorm ticking over, and how it was only my skilful management of the group that got us into that dreamy, trance-like state of harmonious productivity. To which she replied, "No, I think I could do it. I'm a bit of a show-off too."

7. Pick the best

When that phase of the brainstorm is done, you need to go through and sort out the best ideas. It's often useful to remind people of the brief at this point, so that they're thinking about what will work and not just what they like. I get each person to make their own shortlist from all the names the group has come up with. Usually between five and seven works best. They then report back to the whole group on their favourites, and we see where they overlap. Getting people to do it individually first stops the loud or more senior people influencing the others too much. You can then discuss the shortlist, and the shortlist within the shortlist that the group's overlapping preferences have thrown up. Now's the time for evaluation. Are there problems we haven't considered with this name we all like? The benefit of doing it this way is that the favoured names already have a body of support behind them while they're being discussed. Again, this just seems to make the atmosphere healthier – the aim is to be realistic about some names we know people like rather than to look for the negative in an idea that someone's just had.

I also put a limit on how many names people can shortlist that they came up with themselves. We all think our ideas are the best, because they're the product of how our individual minds work. It's then too easy to think they are intrinsically, logically right. David Gaglione of Landor says:

Those who create a name can usually see the genius in their own name candidates. The key is convincing others. It is critical for a namer to put themselves in the shoes of target audiences, the client, and, often, their colleagues.

Shortlisting like this will give people an honest view on whether a name they came up with appeals to anyone else in the world. But it does also give the opportunity for people to sell in an idea they feel has been overlooked. A word of warning. People will always claim they can't remember which names they came up with. Nonsense. They know. And as soon as people repeat in a shortlisting session a name they said in the actual brainstorm, everyone else knows too. We remember hearing the word coming out of their mouth.

So, what's the point of workshops structured in this way? Well, the main stated aim is to come up with lots of ideas, and it certainly works for that. In fact, you'll probably come up with hundreds. Oddly, by far the largest number of names comes out in the first couple of hours of a brainstorm, when you can fairly easily come up with a few hundred ideas. But there's definitely a law of diminishing returns, and even in a day's worth of naming I don't think I've had a group come up with a thousand names.

So a brainstorm will help you come up with names: some good ones, and some shockers. In terms of a rate of return for good ones, you'll do much better out of a namer than a brainstorm. Although I have run brainstorms that have ended up with the name of products: Frescato, a name for Costa Coffee's cold coffee drink (read "Frappuccino" competitor) and TianTian, a super duper health drink in the UK (you get it by mail order, oddly). In the first, we were looking for a made up word that suggested freshness (and sounded Italian). And in the second, we were trying to give a sense of oriental wisdom behind the product, and someone piped up that they knew the Chinese for "daily" and TianTian was born. Interestingly, neither of these names was thought up by the "creatives" in the room. One was from the strategy consultant on the job, and one from the project manager. Which really does go to show that anyone can come up with the winning name.

But the brainstorm has a couple of other secret benefits. First, if you make it fun, it will help you bond as a team – particularly if there's a mix of clients and agency. Everyone gets to show a bit of their personality in a slightly more relaxed situation than the usual stuffy old meetings. The clients also get to have a bit of the fun they think is going on all the time at the agency (it's not; they're sitting there worrying about how soon they can invoice the client). Síne Old of brand consultancy Dave says:

The biggest mistake people make in a naming is not allowing themselves to enjoy the process. How often do you get a chance to sit in a room or in a park and think of ways you would like to have your company or your products discussed? To have the time to imagine what you want people to feel when they hear the name for the first time? To allow yourself the time to try to experience your company by how your name will look and feel to your customers' ears and eyes? It is fantastic fun – enjoy the experience.

It's also good for buy-in to the process, particularly if you can get the key decision makers there. It means everyone has been part of it. If you're lucky, you might also have shown them that it's harder than they think (if they've found it tough just to come up with names in the first place, or if no one has ended up shortlisting the names they thought up). It can also get the bigwigs used to the idea nice and early that their opinion isn't necessarily right – after all, it's unlikely in the shortlisting that their choices will be exactly the same as those of the entire group.

Most professional namers can come up with hundreds of names on their own, just writing them down on pieces of paper in front of them. Of course, sitting at a desk in an office (even the rather swankily furnished and expensively feng-shuied offices of an international brand consultancy) is probably not going to be the best place to come up with ideas, however well stocked with biscuits it may be. So naming, whether client-side or agency-side, actually gives you a fantastic excuse to get out of the office. I always found that it was good to keep moving; after more than about an hour and a half in one place you tend to have absorbed all the creative stimulus that you are going to get from it. Just move on to another. In fact, lots of my best ideas have come on the buses and the Tube around London on my way to and from places, particularly after an initial briefing meeting. Most namers do their best work pretty soon after the briefing. Maybe that's why Síne Old says:

The secret of getting a good name into the world is as complex, exciting, and simultaneously mundane as a band having a good song released – you write, dream, hypothesize and rewrite, wordsmith some more, and then get it back to the idea you thought of in the five minutes after your first client meeting.

In the time after that, there's the diminishing returns again. Sometimes it helps to find somewhere that somehow ties into the spirit you're trying to come across in the name (go and name a 4x4 in some rugged country park, that's my advice to you). Sometimes it works just to have a change of scene. Working at Interbrand in London's Covent Garden was great, because we could sneak down to the side of the Thames, go and sit in the National Gallery or walk to the Great Court of the British Museum, have a cup of coffee in Trafalgar Square, or maybe just lounge on the grass of the local churchyard. It's fun. Heck, even writing about it is quite fun. Have pad and pen, and namer will travel. The worst thing about the dot com era was that it tied us lusty creatives to our desks, so that we could check if absurd names like wildmoosechase.com had been registered. These were the days before the dawn of wi-fi.

I don't believe the namer needs too many things to help them – after all, most names have to resonate with a wide number of people. It's likely that the ideas behind those names will be lurking somewhere in the popular consciousness, which we all carry round in our heads. So, you should be able to pull most good naming ideas kicking and screaming out of your own psyche, without resorting to reference material. It is useful to have a dictionary, of course, and a good thesaurus is useful to stop you getting stuck in a rut. Sometimes there's one word that a brief triggers in your head, and you end up basing all your names on it. So finding the alternative is useful. You just have to be careful you don't end up using a really odd alternative that no one else but Roget has ever heard of. For names that depend on stories, things like encyclopaedias of mythology and legend can be great, as can big atlases (or maybe I just like being surrounded by nice books). Again though, you need to be careful not to be seduced into really ugly sounding words because they have a great rationale behind them (which you'll never get the chance to tell the end consumer) or creating really beautiful names by fusing together those of utterly random or irrelevant mythical beings.

Of course, these days, the young whippersnapper kids of naming will be doing all of this on Google. It's great that there is such a ready source of information on nigh on everything in the world (and I know someone who's written a good book on this, if you're interested) but again, for the moment, it could keep them sitting unhelpfully in the office for too long.

Which, in fact, neatly brings us to the thorny question of the use of technology in naming. Branding consultancies have made their money on naming by employing graduates like me with no experience of the real world, because you don't really need any experience to sit there and think up a few good names. And of course, that was good news for the occasionally shaky agency P&Ls, because you can charge quite a lot for naming, while the people doing it are relatively cheap in the scheme of an agency. Which means nice high margins. But of course, they're not daft, these companies. If it's that easy, surely you could just get computers to do it? Admittedly they have even less experience of the real world, but then they're even cheaper (and they won't try and take money for a pension off you 20 years later, either). Indeed, various people have flirted with using computers for naming.

Now, let's be fair to them. Computers are much better at some kinds of specific naming jobs than real people like me. Occasionally we would get scary briefs from pharmaceutical companies with very, very specific requirements, "We need a seven letter word where the second letter is X and the last one is Q." Or, "Give us every combination of letters that starts VOLTA-, has two letters in the middle, and ends in L." I'm not kidding. You can imagine how a namer's heart sinks when faced with a brief like that. Now the computer will produce answers to these questions very quickly. Most of what it spews out will be unpronounceable gibberish, but get a real person to look through the list; they'll quickly spot the contenders that could work as names, probably much more quickly than they would have come up with all of those names. So use your computer if you want a name that looks like a very dodgy Scrabble hand.

There are more cunning things you can do, though. You can put all the names you've ever thought of for anything into a database, alongside the key elements of the brief that went with it. You see, there are only so many briefs out there. Even products which are entirely different, and in entirely different categories, can be marketed as having similar benefits. So, when you get a similar brief to one you worked on six months before, you can go back to the database and trawl through all the names you thought of earlier.

The problem is the software just isn't subtle enough at the moment. Very poor quality control. It doesn't get the nuances of what might make a name work on one project and not another. So you end up with a very bored namer, reading long lists of computer printouts, looking for the one shining needle in the haystack. In my experience, on any brief, real people have always come up with the best names. Because, for now at least, only people can make the really exciting creative leap, the link between one thing and another, or the sideways view of something that leads to a really interesting unusual name. And the other thing is that most clients are excited by the prospect of having a creative person pondering their needs, having a flash of inspiration, and arriving at something great (even if it doesn't always happen quite that easily). Telling them you're just getting a computer to analyse some data to name their business baby just isn't that inspiring. So after a while, at Interbrand, we decided to never mention the computer again. I don't think it did us any harm. But maybe the day of technology will come. Never say never. But for now, stick to a real person.

8

"the **maybe** names can be your saviour"

Let the show begin

SO, YOU'VE GOT YOUR SWANKY LIST OF NAMES. How do you present them to the people who are going to have to make the decision, and get them to choose? You'd think the hard work would be done by now. But I think this is the toughest bit of naming. This is the bit where your beautifully nurtured names are exposed to the true craziness of your colleagues' or clients' subjectivity. Why is it so tricky? I think there are a number of reasons:

1. We all use language, so we all feel qualified to comment on it

Language works because it's owned by all of us. Somehow, we all sort of agree what something means, and if we all stick to the agreement, then language works. Of course that agreement can change over time. That's what causes language to evolve, and old fuddy-duddies to be constantly grumbling on in the press about the supposedly parlous state of the tongue. (They've been grumbling about the same thing for hundreds of years, and it hasn't made the blindest bit of difference.) For instance, at the moment in English, the agreement over what "disinterested" means is changing. For most people, it used to mean "impartial." Now most of us use it to mean the same as "uninterested." There's nothing very extraordinary about that – it seems to be falling into line with other words like "dissatisfied" and "displeased" where the word with "dis-" at the beginning means the opposite of the word without it. And really, it's no great problem. We still have words like impartial (and dispassionate!) to help us get our message across. But without any one person making the decision, the agreement has changed.

Anyway, the reason behind this semi-rant is simply that because language belongs to all of us, most people feel very qualified to comment on it. What's tricky is that we're not very good at drawing the line as to which bits of linguistic comment require specialist knowledge and which don't; after all, I'm very good at breathing – I've done it successfully for 29 years now – but I wouldn't be able to regale you with my opinions on respiratory biology, the way some people do with language. Thus speaks the embittered linguistics graduate, whose subject nearly everyone thinks they know.

So when you present people with ideas for names, they rarely have nothing to say. We're used to doing it, after all – people choose names for their own children, and comment on it when their friends call their children Augustus or Myfanwy. Sophie Devonshire talks about it like this:

The most difficult bit of naming is definitely the subjectivity of it all. The best example of this has got to be trying to name your unborn child. I thought it would be one of the most fun bits of being pregnant, but it was really hard. I didn't take the established route of not discussing it with people, mind. Tom and

I discussed it with everyone! It was quite fun, hearing different people's likes and dislikes. We were working in Dubai at the time, so it was particularly interesting in a multicultural environment to have the Arabs suggesting Jawaher and Fatima and the Kiwis going for Kentons and Walkers and the fools-that-are-our-friends suggesting things like Sandy (because of the desert). The really interesting thing though, as I was trying to name a company at work and a child at home, was the subjectivity. I'd find a fabulous name that worked well with Tom's surname, and then he'd shoot it down because it reminded him of a dog he once knew. Or I had an irrational hatred of a couple of names that "sounded fat." Of course it was the same at work as we presented the dramatic and different and fabulous names for renaming the company and our dear Lebanese client just said, "Nope, that's not my company."

All of this puts the professional namer in an odd position. You're employed for some kind of level of linguistic knowledge or creativity with words, but when it comes to discussing and picking names, somehow clients forget that they've employed you for your expertise. They rarely take your opinion into account if they really disagree with it. Oh well, such is the namer's lot. There's nothing to do but grin and bear it. Or write a book and complain about it.

2. We all have emotional reactions to words and sounds

It really is extraordinary how strongly people react to names. Because we're using language all the time, words, bit of words, and even sounds have emotional resonances for people. The difficult bit in getting people to judge names is getting them to decide which of the reactions they're having are entirely subjective – it's an association that they have, but maybe only them – and which are more generally shared. Obviously the bigger the number of people you ask, the clearer an answer you'll get to that, but frankly you certainly don't want all those people sitting in your naming meeting poring over your every idea. The best you can hope for is to make people aware of the danger of their own rampant subjectivity and try to get them to manage it. Mathew Weiss, senior planner at branding agency Coley Porter Bell says:

The hardest bit of naming is staying objective. It's virtually impossible not to infer your own personal experiences and prejudices on to the meaning and suitability of name. It's like naming your first born. Objectively Poppy is a pretty name for a girl, but if you knew a fat heifer at school called Poppy it's a no-no, and no one's going to persuade you otherwise.

At Interbrand, we used to have a name for this disease. We called it "Grandma's Cat Syndrome," after the tendency of people to say, "Well, the name's OK, but my grandma had a cat called that, and it died a bit gruesomely in a car accident on the road into town, so I could never call my brand that." Sophie might call it Tom's Dog Syndrome. OK, we never had exactly that situation. But we certainly had the situation where the chief executive's wife or secretary (who may or may not also have been his wife – or mistress) took objection to a name for no very clear reason, and he would listen to her RATHER THAN TO US. Extraordinary! Mentioning the symptoms of Grandma's Cat Syndrome before a potential name has even passed your lips is helpful. If you're really lucky, it will get the participants of the meeting actually policing themselves – "Oh shut up, that really is Grandma's Cat, mate!" – so that you don't have to do it. It just makes them a little more critical about their own responses. And that's a big help.

3. A name can't do everything

Yes, I know I can't keep going on about this one, but it really is the thing people need to get into their heads. A naming presentation is basically an hour and a half of managing someone's expectations.

I spend at least the first half hour making people depressed: I say the name can communicate one or two things at most, so they need to decide quick which are the one or two things they'd like their name to say; that most of the most famous brand names on the planet aren't that great; that names need design, straplines, advertising and communications to bring them to life; and that most new brand names are thought odd or useless when they first arrive.

At this point people are usually almost giving up on the whole process, and have had just about had it up to here with all the preliminaries and are gagging to say the names. These two states are great for the presenter, because it means the names usually come as a pleasant relief. When they see a few names they actually like, people are ecstatic, because you've prepared them for such abject misery. The "it doesn't say such and such" comments you get then are fairly easily batted away. Those comments are actually usually ways of finding seemingly rational reasons for what are really more emotional, subjective reactions to a name, in any case. But you need to get to the root of the real objections, rather than trying to deal with the intellectual smokescreens people tend to put up.

4. You can seldom "tweak" a name to make it work better

Names are pretty simple things. Usually a collection of just a few letters and sounds, a few words at most. Unlike, say, design, which has a large number of elements (for instance colour, shape, texture, typeface, photography, and so on), there isn't much to a name. If a piece of design work feels almost there, but not quite, there are lots of things you can do to tweak it, to move it closer to what you're actually looking for. That's virtually impossible with a name, especially if you're dealing with real names. You can't say, "Orange. Hmm. Jeez, that's almost right, how about we make it Oringe? Yeah, that seems better." They feel either right or wrong, which again makes choosing a name feel quite brutal.

Names are very easy to reject. I work on the principle that 50 per cent of the names I suggest on any project will be rejected by the decision-makers; it just seems to be the ratio that people need to get to feel like they've exercised their executive opinion. You can't get precious about this. You need to know that some of the names you're presenting are always going to be sacrificial lambs, slaughtered at the corporate altar. You have to not see this is a criticism of your work; it's a process they need to go through to help them feel comfortable. In fact, it's helpful to you as a namer. Allowing people to see what they don't like – and to reject it – actually makes them feel more positive about the names they do. They become their favourites (and of course, if you're a bit of a ham, like I am, you'll actually play this up to exaggerate the warm feeling they have towards their new favourite names, and to your work).

It's also one of the reasons why a naming process can get harder as it goes on. In the initial phase, when you're looking at a wide range of names, people can usually decide fairly clearly which naming territory – and the names that go with it – they like and which they don't. As the process goes on, in theory at least, the brief gets honed so that more of the names are in the right territory. That means it actually gets harder for people to decide which names they prefer. In terms of pure logic, this is a good thing; because naming is such a numbers game, intellectually you're looking for a set of names that do roughly the same job, so that when legal and linguistic screening do their worst, it doesn't matter which live and which die. But in terms of how happy the client is, it can be a bit of a problem. They often like the clear-cut yes and no phase, because it's quite exciting (most of us enjoy feeling things strongly, and getting the opportunity to express our opinion. Or is that just me?). As it goes on, and the names get more similar, their reactions become less emotional. Sometimes the clients themselves interpret this as a sense of being underwhelmed; that maybe the names they thought they liked aren't that good after all; that generally the process has lost its sparkle.

How do you deal with this? It's difficult. I've found the best thing to do is to warn them in advance about the impending lull. Then if it happens, you can rationalize it to them, and maybe stop them having quite so much of a wobble (though even that doesn't always work). If they don't get the wobble, then they probably just don't even think about it ever again.

5. Maybe is good

This is a hard lesson for people to accept. But there will be names to which people react entirely neutrally; they just can't decide if they like them or not. Naturally a namer's ego is slightly disappointed at that point; after all, it's slightly upsetting if the only reaction to your pearls of wisdom is a shrug of the shoulders and a funny little "hmmmph" noise. But "maybe" can be a good reaction. Often the same names can get very positive or very negative reactions from different people – it means they can be very polarizing. Orange and Monday are examples of names that did exactly that. But not every organization is brave enough for one of those polarizing kinds of names.

In which case, the maybe names can be your saviour. They succeed because no one really objects to them. And Sod's Law has it that those are the names that somehow manage to sneak through linguistic searches, through legals, through the customer research, and through the chief exec's secretary. These names are the unsung heroes of the naming world. The dull ones. The plodders. Not stylish. But they get the job done. I mean, do you think anyone was ever really excited by the name Microsoft? Come on now.

6. It's artificial

The people making these decisions need constant reminding that discussing names for any length of time at all (as they'll have to come to a decision) is an entirely artificial situation. The same applies if they go on to ask real customers what they think in research, as we'll see. People just won't think of names in this detail in real life. So if it takes them ten minutes to come up with some negative connotation or association of a name, then probably no one in real life will ever come up with it.

As I've said, there are lots of businesses who really don't need the help of agencies and consultants to help them come up with names – with enough people, and enough time, and by running things in the right way – most of us would be able to come up with enough good names for whatever it is we wanted to name. But it's this bit – managing the slightly unexpected impact of weird human nature on what should be a fairly normal business process – where a bit of experience really, really helps.

So how can you present names for consideration by a group of people to help manage this without ending up tearing out your hair? Here are a few rules:

1. Don't allow too long for the meeting

As with naming generally, these kinds of discussions and decisions can go on forever if you let them (and you don't want them to; people will talk themselves out of every name, even the ones they really loved when they first saw them).

2. Don't have too many people in the meeting

This is the opposite of the rule for brainstorms. Otherwise it turns into a free for all, and there'll be someone who'll find a problem with every name. About five is the maximum, in my book. Ideally, you want the most important decision makers in the room. An hour to an hour and a half is plenty.

3. Set the rules before you start

Again, you're looking for ways to manage (and take charge of) the way people respond to the names. So tell them they're not allowed to worry about Grandma's Cat. Tell them that maybes are good. Most importantly, make them keep their reactions to themselves until you've shown them all the names. Firstly, it helps them to get a sense of the whole set of names before they give their reactions. But also it stops names being knocked out and left to float, dead in the water before everyone's eyes, in the middle of the presentation (which can really take the energy out of the room, too).

4. Never, never, never just show the names

Because the situation of choosing names is so artificial, you need to fall over yourself to give the names some real life context: logos, business cards, mocked-up headlines in the *Wall Street Journal* featuring the company's name. As Glyn Britton of Albion says:

Brand names are funny. What you thought about them at first isn't what you think about them now. Many of them take on new meanings as a result of years of personal experience and marketing effort. The classic of course is Virgin, which stands for a lot of things but not the obvious thing. So, in order to assess a potential name, you have to try and project forward five years. You need to picture the experiences you may have with this company in that time. You need to imagine the effect of the marketing they may do in that time. You need to understand if the name has longevity or will it quickly date. And, crucially, you have to try and do this from the position of your mum – someone who doesn't understand or care much about your clever creative idea, but just goes shopping.

To help clients do this, you do need to be a little bit of a salesman. I like to talk through each name – not for long, thirty seconds or so – so that people understand the thought process behind the name, and have it brought to life a little. The secret here is not to get carried away. Obviously if the name only works when you've given a five minute rationale about its classical roots, then it's probably not a very good name. After all, you're not going to get a chance to do your spiel in the aisles of Wal-Mart or on the floor of the stock exchange.

5. Let everyone else give their opinion before the boss

If you don't, there are always some oily little oiks who'll only say what the boss says, and he or she might well be wrong. So I find it helps to get people to say what they think before the boss does, so he or she can see if he or she is completely outnumbered. That will be an eye-opener for some bosses. Others, of course, will flatly ignore it.

6. Allow yourself to push a few favourites

Let's say you've got 20 to 25 names to present (that's the sort of number I usually aim for). Now some of the names will be names that you absolutely love. A few, probably. The rest you probably think do the job strategically. Some you will know are just there as makeweights, if you're honest. What happens if your real favourites don't make the final cut? Well, I think it depends how definitively they've been rejected. Assuming they weren't just utterly dissed from the minute your audience set eyes on them, you can probably do something to rescue them. In each set of that many names, I've found you can probably force one or two through with sheer charm, and what there is of the "naming expertise" card. Weirdly, it almost works best if you don't try to justify your favouritism too much. If you try to explain to someone why a name they're umming and ahhhing about is a great name, you rarely persuade them with logic. Instead you need to get them with an emotional punch.

Usually for me, that means just saying, "That's a great name. Just trust me. I've been doing this for years, and that's a great name. You'd be mad to knock it out." More often than not, it works.

7. Never, never, never include any joke names

OK, OK, I know this sounds obvious to you. But to me it always seems like a good idea at the time. And as a result I've had my fingers severely burnt. In the process of coming up with names for something, there are always some that you think are just great gags. They make you chuckle, and you think to yourself, why, that would make my client chuckle too. It'll help build our rapport to share a wee joke together. It'll show them I'm human. It'll be great. Er, no. They either: a) think you've been wasting their time and money thinking up joke names and stop taking you seriously (fair enough, really, when you put it like that) or, and probably worse, b) they actually take you seriously. This is especially bad if you present it in the middle of a list of perfectly good names, with an equally convincing, and to you, hilarious spiel. I've done it. Often they end up quite liking the name, and you have to sheepishly admit to them that actually, terribly sorry, that one won't really work. I was just having a laugh. Not only does it make them feel stupid, but it makes them suspicious of the whole process. After all, if you had them fooled with that one, how do they know the rest isn't also all a load of old cobblers? They begin to think you're just a silver-tongued rogue talking them into buying a whole wardrobe of the emperor's new clothes. Not good.

8. Warn them of the ups and downs

We've talked about the slightly deflating sense clients can get as a naming process goes on, and how letting them know what's going to happen can only help. But it's also good to warn them about how people tend to feel about names for the next few days after they've first encountered them. Although I do get people to give "snap" reactions to names in meetings (and often they end up being the most genuine and useful reactions to names, because they're most like the reactions people have in real life), it is useful to get people also to take a couple of days to dwell on them.

Partly it's useful because you can show people that it's easy to get used to a name. As we've seen with Zeneca, unless a name actually has some terrible association attached to it, people learn to live with most names, and do business perfectly happily under them. People come to live with them, especially if they're in some kind of context. I know most namers have experienced that feeling of utter frustration when they see a name a client had initially reacted to fairly neutrally – even negatively – starting to soar in their estimation as soon as some designer has come along and written it in a brightly coloured shape. It just has so much more resonance for people (and it's exactly what happened with Ocado, for instance).

Before you get to this stage of somewhat resigned acceptance though, there's usually a couple of days after the names are first discussed, when clients get a little sinking feeling, when they think all the names have something wrong with them, and they start to despair. Another day, and some, usually the good ones, will start to creep back up in their estimation. Again, it pays to warn them. If it doesn't happen, you've not lost a sausage, and if it does, you can reassure them their reactions are perfectly normal, and they haven't actually been saddled with a load of duff names.

9. Pull a few tricks

Sneaky one, this. But it can be quite handy to jolt your audience awake mid-presentation to the slightly ludicrous arbitrariness of trying to name a brand – to make them realize that although it's important, they need to keep it in perspective, and that it's not the be all and end all. How can you do that? Well how about sticking the names Coca-Cola or Kodak in the middle? Suddenly, when seen alongside other ideas, they are shown up for what they are. There's nothing intrinsically brilliant about them. They did not have success written all over them. Coca-Cola in particular is a really quite odd collection of letters, with what sounds like quite a rude word at the beginning (and launched at a time when every other product was called Something-Cola). Showing that these names are not gods of the brand pantheon, but mere mortals, sets of sounds like all the others, helps show people that it's really not just the name you choose, but what you do with them that counts. It helps people to see that familiarity is nine-tenths of brand success, and that the unfamiliarity of new ideas shouldn't lead them to be too sceptical about their potential.

9

"a name that sounds beautiful to my ears might sound like a right old **clanger** to yours "

The language barrier

OF COURSE COMING UP WITH GREAT NAMES (or even just mediocre ones) is a creative exercise. But as I've said, it's a numbers game, too. Can you back enough horses so that after several hundred have fallen at the first hurdle, thrown their riders or just inexplicably gone lame, you'll still end with a winner?

One of the most depressing ways of knocking out tons of lovely-sounding names is to do language checks on them. It sounds obvious, but it's amazing how many brands go wrong at this point. The principle is straightforward. Think where your product or company is going to be sold, or do business. Naturally, if you're British, your list of names is going to sound pretty damn groovy in British English. But is the same true in Iceland? Or Iran? Even the differences between English in the UK, US, Canada, Australia, India or anywhere else can be pretty startling, and enough to kill a name stone dead.

So what kills the names? Well, when you've got your list of likely candidates, you need to make sure that each one doesn't look like, or sound like, a word that means something rude or inappropriate in any language of any country where you're likely to be doing business. A good language check will also pick up similarities to any local brand names that you don't know about, without you going to the excruciatingly vast expense of local legal searches (don't worry, we'll get on to my rant about lawyers soon. Hold on to your hats).

As a namer in the UK, who did languages at school and university, I tend to come up with names using the sounds and meanings borrowed from Germanic and Romance languages, so I've got a good idea that my names will probably be OK in French, Italian, Spanish, German, the Scandinavian languages and the like. But I have no idea what resonances they'll have in Slavic languages, or Arabic, or the Chinese languages. It means a name that sounds mellifluously beautiful to my Anglo-Saxon ears – like linguistic spun silk, in fact – might sound like a right old clanger to yours. Aside from learning new languages, the language check is really the only way of finding out.

The simplest way is to get a native speaker to look at and read out a shortlist of names and tell you what they think – any particularly positive or negative connotations that spring to mind. Ideally, that speaker should be living in the country you're interested in, so they're really *au fait* with the language of the moment, and the current cultural climate. In fact, if you can, use 2 or 3 speakers for each country; we're all individuals, and we're all human, so we don't all pick up the same things in new words. That will also give you a sense of how strong the resonances of a particular word are (if you're wobbling because you've not come up with many decent names, and you need every last one you can get). This also helps you get out of the entirely unhelpful situation of a language checker who's so embarrassed by what a name suggests to them, that they won't even tell you what it means. Or worse, they're *so* embarrassed that they don't tell you about it at all. I heard tell of a project where a new name caused quite a stir in the Italian American community, because the Italian checker was uncomfortable flagging up a similarity to the word "rape" in Italian. As a language checker, that counts as being utterly, utterly useless at your job.

Often you can get translation agencies to help with this task if you can't get your hands on native speakers through your company or friends. But take care, dear reader. Be really specific with what you want them to tell you about, and what you don't. It seems that lurking inside many language checkers is a lonely, embittered brand consultant who never got a job. But often they seem to believe your language check is their moment in the sun. The spotlight's on them. We're consulting them. Finally. You don't get a short snappy discussion about the word sounding like the Polish word for "bum" or not. Instead, get ready for a two page tirade about the state of the Polish retail market, and what this person (who's really just an ordinary punter) thinks will go down well with the 70-year-old ladies of Wroclaw. Your brand probably isn't aimed at the 70-year-old ladies of Wroclaw, but have no fear, that won't stop them. You get comments like, "I don't like it." Oh my days, I can't begin to tell you how annoying that is on a language check. You have very likely paid money for the benefit of hearing this person's opinion, and probably had to wait 24 hours for that linguistic opinion, while senior people are breathing down your neck, wondering where that bloody list of names is. AND HE SAYS, "I DON'T LIKE IT!" Why not? Is there anything actually WRONG with it, you jumped-up clot, or is it just your idle prejudice? (I used to frame these questions slightly more politely when I was actually paid to do this, you understand.) An answer probably then takes another 24 hours to come back, probably with more similarly ill-judged pontificating. I'm not using Polish as a hypothetical example, by the way. He knows who he is. We had to get rid of him in the end. Not murdered, of course, but he didn't do many more language checks.

Some languages will seem to cause you endless problems too. For some reason nigh on every name I ever came up with meant something unspeakably, but often brilliantly, inventively rude in Arabic or Hungarian. Or maybe those languages have lots of rude words. Write into my publisher if you speak Arabic or Hungarian and let me know (they'll love that). Even languages you know quite well can take you by surprise. I speak fluent French (with a Québécois accent, which French French speakers always patronizingly tell me is "charming") but could never, ever remember that when we came up with the name Chime (which we often did; it's a really pretty image, a great metaphor for different elements coming together harmoniously), it always makes the French think of "chîmer" – to get drunk. And I would kick myself. Again.

Particular letters can cause most of the problems. There are certain letters that are quite "unstable" in the sense that they represent completely different sounds in different languages. Step forward "J". "J" is the king of these unstable letters. In English it's the sound we know from James Bond and J-Lo. In French, it's the softer sound of "je" and "joue." In Germanic languages, it's usually the "y" sound of Jung. In Spanish languages you'll need to hoik up a lot of phlegm to do the "hchhhh" of Jamón Jamón. X isn't that great either, which is why I still worry about the name Jetix, which we came up with when Fox TV sold their kids' TV brand to Disney, which was, logically, but somewhat inconveniently, called Fox Kids. God knows how Jetix would be pronounced in Hopi.

Personally, I think the need for a name to sound *exactly* the same in every conceivable territory can be overstated, and is just not really feasible anyway, because of how languages work. Heck, it sounds different when me and my mum say Coca-Cola, because her northern English "o" vowel sounds different to my posher southern one. But we can tell we're saying the same word, and that's what matters. There's no communication problem. And naturally, the same applies between languages as well as within them. I mean have you ever heard a French person say Rrrrrrrrrrrrrrrrrrrrrrrrrrrrenault? It's quite a long way from the "REN-oh" us Brits can manage.

You can of course use the fact that a word is difficult to pronounce – because it's from a language that sounds quite different to yours – to your advantage. You can exploit the "nationality" of a name by imbuing your brand with the qualities associated with the country of its origin. Take a name like Wrangler. That beginning, and that consonant cluster of "-ng-", is a complete nightmare to pronounce in lots of languages (especially those like Italian or Japanese which typically follow every consonant with a vowel). But it is unmistakably English (language) in character. It fits with the rough-around-the-edges, all-American authenticity of the brand. In the same vein, people even make made-up names hard to pronounce, like Häagen-Dazs.

The problem with all this, of course, is that often you just don't know where your brand is going to end up doing business five, ten or fifteen years down the line. Underestimate it, and you store up problems for yourself later, by having to use different names in different places, which is unnecessarily expensive. Overestimate it, and you might find yourself rejecting brilliant names because they mean "early autumn" in Inuktitut, or some other language which will probably never make the blindest bit of difference to the numbers on your business plan. And clearly, the bigger your brand, the less you have to worry about odd little meanings in tedious little languages. It took Google a long time to launch a site in Norway, and one of the reasons that's been suggested is that the name Google looks oddly like the word for "glasses" in Norwegian. But by the time Google had become a worldwide mega brand, no one seemed all that bothered. Even in Oslo.

Arguably too, linguistic problems have to be very, very bad indeed to derail a great brand, or a great product. It goes back to the fact that once it's familiar, most of us only really worry about whether we can say a name, rather than what it makes us think of. And if, as some have suggested, it's actually a different bit of our brain that deals with brand names, as opposed to normal words, that helps too. It means that potentially negative-sounding words can be divorced from their negatives. In fact, there's almost some inverse cool from names that stand firm in the face of potential negatives. Smeg are a manufacturer of things like fridges. Big, cool ones (cool in the swinging sixties Carnaby Street sense, rather than the ordinary fridge sense). They've become quite a recherché item for middle class London hipsters, who simply ignore the fact that "smeg" has come to mean "a disgusting substance" in British English (and also a sort of surrogate swearword in the British sci-fi sitcom *Red Dwarf*). But Smeg fridges have done so well among the urban intelligentsia that they're even parodied in the new Wallace and Gromit film, with a fridge that just bears the name Smug.

But there are bigger problems on the way for big brands expanding out of their home markets into countries that don't use the Roman alphabet, or even an alphabet that works on the same principles. Take Mandarin and Cantonese. There, you need to find Chinese characters to represent the sounds of your name (this is called transliteration). The problem is that with Chinese characters, the same sound can have lots of different meanings. So Western brands transforming themselves for the Chinese market need to find a set of meanings that roughly sounds like the original name, and are also appropriate to the brand in some way. My advice to any young graduates who want to make a mint in the next few years is to learn Mandarin and Cantonese, and set yourself up as brand-savvy transliterator. This is a business that's just going to EXPLODE.

This conundrum has led to a new version of the "everything means something terrible in Hungarian and Arabic" problem. Allow me to introduce the "everything means death in Chinese" problem. The multiple meanings of Chinese characters mean it's pretty easy, if you're that way inclined, to read something negative, or at the least nonsensical, into almost any combination of sounds in Chinese. I had a client who was looking for a worldwide name for a product that was going to be marketed in China. His colleague in Shanghai was quite a grumpy old sort, and managed to poo-poo any potential name he personally didn't like, using the "it means death in Chinese" trick. Well, it could. But it could also mean lots of other much more mundane and acceptable things.

The transliteration problem has also led to some of the biggest urban naming myths going. The multiple interpretations of Chinese characters mean you could just about interpret one Chinese version of the name Coca-Cola as meaning, "bite the wax tadpole." To settle the problem, Coke came up with their own version – sounding something like "ko-ka ko-ler" and meaning, "let the mouth be able to rejoice," which is just about absolutely bang on brief for Coke.

All in all, there's a lot of nonsense talked about the perils of language problems with brands. But on the other hand, get it wrong, and it really can cause big problems. And it's something that car brands seem to keep wading into. When GM launched their new all-singing all-dancing supermini a few years ago, they called it the Nova. Redolent of something new and modern in Romance languages. They thought. Actually, to Spanish speakers it just sounded like "don't go." A bit of a problem for a car. Similarly the name of the Toyota MR2 was always going to cause a problem in France. Go on, spell it out for yourselves, French speakers. It sounds like shit, literally. So, in France, the MR2 became the Monsieur 2. Likewise there was always something a little too intrusively medical about the Ford Probe to really make it the pulse-racing sports car success they were hoping for. Hats off to Volkswagen, though, for sticking with the Sharan when it was being pilloried left, right and centre in the British media. The launch came as the UK was obsessed with caricaturing Kevins, Tracys, and Sharons – supposedly archetypal working-class names.

Most of us have seen brand names abroad that seem funny to us. At Interbrand we used to collect these in something called the Black Museum – once a glass cabinet in reception that got relegated to the basement when we realized that people thought it was a showcase of our best work. The same stuff was collected in a book called *Shelf Life*. Everyone has their own favourites. I've always loved Crapsy Fruit cereal (from France), the drink Pocari Sweat (from Japan) and Skum sweets (from Sweden). Of course, chuckling away at these is slightly unfair, as they were never meant for English-speaking markets in the first place. I've actually always harboured a secret ambition to get one of my names in some other country's Black Museum (brilliantly, an American Interbrand colleague once rang from the States to

I Can't Believe It's Not Butter

A name that defies one of the great naming rules, that shorter is better. ICBINB (we're all friends here) is a spread that's not butter, but claims to taste like it. It wears its length as a badge of honour. It's so unwieldy and in your face that it makes itself utterly unforgettable. You'd think its directness would be far too brash for British tastes, but even we have taken it to our hearts.

It goes to show that rules are there to be broken. Yes it's long, but it's all very simple. Compare it to the British design agency Syzygy, whose name is very short, but totally intimidating to say or spell. And what does it mean anyway?

suggest the name Black Museum belonged in the Black Museum itself, lest it be confused with a Centre for African American studies). The Black Museum never failed to raise a chuckle in naming presentations though, and got us fantastic, regular PR. There are some British newspapers that printed virtually the same article about Pschitt drinks every time a big new name was launched. It even got us on *The Generation Game*, the UK's worst game show. Some poor unsuspecting member of the public actually had to sit and guess what Bonka might be (it's coffee, from Spain). Luckily she only had to sit there for two minutes. We were there, if I remember rightly, for four hideously unfunny hours, thanks to British "comic" Jim Davidson.

Sometimes it is not the words themselves but their cultural connotations that can be problematic. When Orange launched in Northern Ireland, it was received rather differently from how it went down in the rest of the UK. For there, orange is a colour strongly associated with the Protestant side of the sectarian divide. To this day I know Northern Ireland Catholics who would never use an Orange phone.

On October 18, 2005, the *Korea Times* reported on some of the problems Korean brands had in the USA:

KIA Motors may just have to sit idle and wait for the Iraqi War to come to an end. KIA Motors [is] making its inroad into the North American market with its Sportage SUV and [is] facing a tricky name game; KIA or K.I.A. is an acronym for "killed in action" in the same spirit of M.I.A. for "missing in action." K.I.A. refers to those who died in battle. Though a military jargon it may be, the term referring to the war dead is hardly contained within the barracks. Some war-themed movies or espionage films often include scenes flashing K.I.A. and M.I.A. stamps in dark reddish ink from the files of secret agents. Lately, mothers identify themselves in such a way as "Proud mom of Lt. Ken Ballad: KIA 5.30.04."

Sometimes the problems aren't even down to a local name being exported. Some markets and regions are inherently complex. Sophie Devonshire, who was a namer in Dubai, says:

I named a number of new brands and products for local Middle Eastern products and services. This is an enormous challenge as often you are talking to a number of different nationalities with their own associations with words and pronunciation problems (the classic one with this is that you will often hear Arab speakers talking about drinking Bebsi as there is no P in the Arabic language – although there is one in Farsi so you'll be fine with Iranians). What is aspirational for Indians may be uninspiring for the Lebanese; the hint of the West may work for Arabs but sound passé for the expat English. The advantage of naming in such a market though is that you can get away with still using real words, as they only need to be trademarked for a small region. So Mosaic is OK for a recruitment company helping find the perfect fit and so is Verve, which was the name we gave the Middle East's premier health and fitness event sponsored by a leading bottled water. That bottled water had name problems itself. Christened Oasis when that still seemed a novel idea in a desert state, it is plagued by gas companies, hotels and shopping centres with the same name. And, in addition, it has two names – Oasis in English and Al Waha in Arabic – which creates an obvious difficulty from time to time. In a country where the Arabs speak English as well, our recommendation was always to come up with one name which could be pronounced and sounded OK in both languages – usually driven by English as English products were more aspirational to Arab speakers than the other way round. The Arab names also tended to be quite unimaginative – for example, Istithmar means Investment and there were about five big and otherwise smart companies happily calling themselves that. Using established words still isn't easy though. We spent a long time considering Verdant for a food company – a lovely name redolent of the green that is such an antidote to the dry dustiness of the Middle East. However, if you check dictionaries carefully you find that some dictionaries include a definition of Verdant as meaning gauche and unsophisticated ... not so great for a company full of pride in its developments.

The spread of English as an international business language has left namers in some countries with a dilemma: to name in their language of origin, or of English? What if the local name is complex to Anglophone ears? The *Korea Times* reports on how Japanese companies went about being named (October 26, 2005):

Japanese businesses have a long tradition of naming their companies after their founder, which is a popular method in the West. But the Japanese are ready to give a name a smart twist for easier pronunciation and wider acceptance in other parts of the world.

Like Honda or Hitachi, Japanese words are already easier to pronounce due to the hard sounds and clipped nature of the language. As a result, Japanese corporate logos are more easily recognized and promoted in overseas markets. Nonetheless, some Japanese firms spared no sweat to make their names more effective and memorable with an international look.

Just look at the mammoth car company Toyota. Although the founding family name is Toyoda, the company name was changed to simplify the pronunciation from its birth in 1937.

Mazda Motor was originally known as Matsuda, named for its founder, Jujiro Matsuda. To increase the car's popularity outside of Japan, the company changed its official name to Mazda in 1984 although their cars had been manufactured under the Mazda brand since their first model, Mazdago, was rolled out in 1931.

Moreover, the tyre company Bridgestone was founded by Shojiro Ishibashi in 1931. The surname Ishibashi literally means "a bridge made of stone." Optical instrument giant Canon was founded under a local name in 1933. It adopted the current name in 1935 after the brand name of the company's first camera, the Kwannon, the Japanese name for the Buddhist bodhisattva of mercy.

Beyond the level of simply modifying spelling, some Japanese companies went as far as adopting ordinary English words or Western-style monikers, and their decision to adopt a Western name paid off. Perhaps the best example is Sony, derived from the Latin word for sound. Sony founder Akio Morita had said that he changed the company name from Tokyo Tsushin Kogyo meaning "Tokyo Communication Industry" to Sony because "we were sonny boys working in sound and vision." And the word could be pronounced in any language.

Consumer electronics company Sharp derived from its first product, the Ever-Ready Sharp mechanical pencil, which was invented by its founder, Tokuji Hayakawa, in 1915. On top of that, the list could go on and on with such companies as Pioneer, Olympus, Pentax and Epson.

Arguably, there was a tendency for the first Japanese brands to hide their nationality behind English names when they ventured abroad. In fact, the sign of the desirability of a country's own brand, if we accept such a thing can exist, might be reflected in the acceptability of its native names beyond its own borders. Now that IBM has sold its ThinkPad laptop business to Chinese company Lenovo, that's a name we'll be seeing more and more of in the West. But we'll know that China has really arrived on the international business scene when a name that sounds really Chinese – beyond the realms of alternative medicine – really succeeds on its own terms.

10

"in theory the lawyers are there to protect you from **bigger upsets** later"

The long arm of the law

hurdle, there is a true grim reaper in the world of naming. But this grim reaper does not wear a cloak, nor carry a scythe. Instead he (usually he) is wearing a double-breasted chalk stripe suit, a silk tie with far too large a knot, shiny black brogues, and he has probably gone to lunch already (and as I write, it's only ten o'clock in the morning). The grim reaper is a trademark lawyer (and apologies at this point, to the language sticklers, who probably want me to spell trademark as two words. What can I tell you? I'm a dangerously avant garde naming maverick).

From the namer's point of view, it's his job to pick off your best names, until the last few standing are the ugly ones, or the bland and unadventurous, the names you never liked in the first place. And soon, once he works his black magic, even they will be looking sickly, slightly beaten, unsteady on their feet.

To be fair, he might see his job differently. He might think he's character building. Testing the mettle of potential candidates, to see if they're strong enough for the fight in the outside world. If they can't take him on, they'll never be able to look after themselves.

But why do we need trademark lawyers in the first place? It's a question I've asked myself lots on dark days before naming presentations as lists of 100 great ideas get whittled down to a dodgy-looking 17 names. In theory at least, the lawyers are there to inflict short term pain but to protect you from bigger upsets later.

Trademarks are there, of course, to protect brands, and the people who buy them. To stop one person pretending their stuff is actually someone else's, so that customers don't get confused. And a trademark needn't be just a name. It can be a whole phrase (straplines like Apple's "think different"), a logo, a colour (think of the green of BP petrol stations), sounds (like sonic logos, or advertising jingles), even the smells of perfumes. In short, almost anything that a brand can associate with its products and services, and use as "shorthand" for them, is up for grabs in trademark terms. If they are distinctive enough, they can be registered in isolation from each other, or registered in conjunction with one another (thereby making elements which are less distinctive in themselves recognizable as a package).

Arguably, the name is the most important bit of that package. You want to make damn sure that no one can come along and just copy the name you're using. Trademarks are a sure fire way of doing it. And the more you use a trademark – the more famous your brand becomes – the more protection you get. Because the better known you are, the easier it is to suggest that competitors would actually gain a significant commercial advantage by associating themselves, deliberately or not, with your brand.

And to clear up a confusion lots of my clients have, when they start out on the road to their brand name, trademarks are not the same as company names, or domain names. In the UK, for instance, when you're setting up a company, you go and register it at a place called Companies House. All they want to know is that your company doesn't have exactly the same name as someone else's. But there doesn't need to be much in it. Neil Taylor Limited, Neil Taylor Holdings Limited, Neil Taylor Writing Limited, and Neil Taylor Million Selling Business Books Limited can all happily co-exist. Your company name is largely a way of helping the authorities keep one corporate entity distinct from another.

But your company name doesn't need to be the same as the brand name you trade under; in fact it might be entirely different. So the mobile phone brand 3 is operated in the UK by Hutchison 3G UK. What this also means is that knowing there is no company registered with the same name as the one you want (or finding a name that's a whisker away from someone else's but still able to be registered) is no guarantee that you'll actually end up being able to use that name in the real world. There might be another company lurking out there with a different name that already owns the trademark you want.

And finding your name is free as a .com (or .co.uk, or .co. jp) or whatever is great news from a business point of view – it means people will be able to find you quickly and easily on what is now a major information and sales channel. But in trademark terms it means nothing. Nada. Zip. Getting the domain name means you're lucky, and nothing else. It's no defence if someone comes along and challenges your use of what they think of as their name.

From the point of view of the naming process, that's what all this fretting about the law really comes down to; can someone else stop you using the name you want to use? If you start using a name that someone else has trademark rights to – if you infringe their rights, in the jargon – then that can be an embarrassing and costly mistake. The worst that can happen is that you're served with something like an immediate order to "cease and desist" using your name. If you're a small company and you get caught out, maybe that's not so bad; sure, you might have to reprint your stationery. But the bigger you are, the worse it is. Think how much time, effort and money gets spent on big brand marketing launches. Think of the cost of informing your hard-won customers that you're changing your name? And think of the effect on your business if, when you change your name, they never find you again.

There are some pretty big brands that have blundered into some big trademark-related problems. And of course, if such cases drag on, the cost of the protracted disputes themselves can be quite crippling. You know how much lawyers charge! How else do you think they afford those chalk stripe suits and long, early lunches? The computer brand Apple has spent many years in litigation with Apple Corps (naming jokes, I love 'em), the record company set up by The Beatles, over the rights to that name. For many years, both sides had a harmonious agreement to coexist with the same name, as long as each didn't veer into the territory of the other's operations. Which was of course fine, until the worlds of music and computers collided. When Apple Computer started using its brand to promote its music software iTunes, and music hardware iPod, the Apple Corps turned from green to red, arguing that Apple Computer had reneged on a deal to steer clear of the world of music with their trademark.

As I write this book, Google has been prevented from using the name Gmail for its e-mail service in the UK, following a similar decision in Germany. In both these countries, while continuing to fight its corner, Google has backed down, and said that new users will be introduced to Googlemail rather than

Gmail. The reason they've had to change? A software company had already registered the name Gmail in these territories, and argues that the products themselves are similar enough to cause confusion. Here's how the story was reported in *Freelance UK* (October 26, 2005):

Google could be forced to give up its Gmail brand across Europe after voluntarily dropping it in the UK, following a trademark dispute with Independent International Investment Research (IIIR), the quoted financial information service.

The dominant search site has begun issuing new users email addresses that end "googlemail.com" after it refused to bow to "exorbitant" demands from a company claiming to own the Gmail name.

London-based IIIR says it used Gmail to describe the Web mail function of its Pronet financial analytics software since May 2002 – two years before Google named its email service.

After the California giant rolled out the first accounts of its email product in April 2004, emblazoned with the Gmail name, Shane Smith, IIIR's CEO, filed a trademark application in the US for the name Gmail.

Smith then contacted Google in June, claiming to own the rights to Gmail and seeking a "business solution" to settle the dispute over the trademark, worth between £27m and £36m according to an independent valuation.

Google disputes Smith's "tenuous" claim to be the owner of the Gmail name and stated, "We are still working with the courts and trademark office to ensure our ability to use the Gmail name, but this could take years to resolve, and in the meantime, we want our users to have an email address and experience they can rely on."

Shane Smith said, "We are a gnat biting the ankle of a giant but that shouldn't stop us defending the intellectual property rights of our shareholders."

Intriguingly, neither of these brands may end up winning the day. *Freelance UK* went on to say (October 26, 2005):

Mike Lynd, a partner at Marks & Clerk, the patent and trademark lawyers, said, "Earlier this year, Google lost the right to use Gmail in Germany, following a dispute with Daniel Giersch of Hamburg who had registered Gmail with the German Patent Office in 2000 ..."

"Though IIIR, Google, and a few hopeful opportunists have rushed to file a Community [EU] Trademark for the Gmail mark, Mr Giersch's existing German registration will undermine all of these applications," Mr Lynd told *The Times*.

Marketing directors should probably pause here for a scary moment and think of the potential consequences of changing the name of a product or service you've spent years to trying to promote.

Another long-running fight is over Budweiser. There are two Budweisers, one US, and one Czech, both named after the Czech town of Ceske Budejovice, or Budweis in German. In 1876, Adolphus Busch picked it as the name of his new beer. Without either side knowing, the Czech company started brewing there in 1895, calling their beer Budweiser Budvar. It's a toughie, of course. Both brands make very, very similar products, and even have a similar claim to the historical origin of their names. So, they are locked in a slow battle over who gets to use the name Budweiser in different territories.

Even if you end up settling a case with someone who claims the same name as you, the publicity surrounding the case can be damaging. A few years ago, British Telecom's mobile arm was rebranded as O_2 before being sold off. The name is supposed to suggest that communication is as essential to life as oxygen, the chemical symbol for which is O_2. A little bit pretentious, I know. But tied to a visual identity showing bubbles of air travelling through water, it actually ended up producing quite a distinctive brand. A very big marketing launch was almost immediately soured by a trademark dispute with the O_2 Centre in North London, a large shopping centre containing things like mobile phone shops. Not only were the names identical, but visually their logos look quite similar, too. And of course, the phone brand's plans included O_2 branded shops. The O_2 Centre argued people were likely to be confused between the two, and the dispute hit the papers, making O_2 and their branding agency look distinctly like they hadn't done their homework. Even today, with the two brands agreeing to coexist, as you come past the O_2 Centre on the train, it still looks like it might be sponsored by the other, now more famous, brand.

Of course, the less distinctive your name, the more likely you are to end up with people with a name very close to yours. Sorry to get on my old rant again, but this is particularly likely to happen with initials. Because the names end up being very short, it's almost odds-on that someone else will have picked the same set of dull old letters to represent something entirely, and maybe embarrassingly, different. The daddy of these battles is over the initials WWF. In the black and white corner, the Worldwide Fund for Nature, the nature protection charity, replete with cuddly panda as its logo. And if you're thinking to yourself it doesn't feel like those initials quite fit together, you'd be right. WWF used to stand for World Wildlife Fund, before they decided their remit extended beyond "wildlife." So the initials that this dispute is about are even a little fudged in the first place. In the gold lamé corner, the World Wrestling Federation, the hilariously camp US attempt at primetime entertainment wrestling. Who owns these letters? Should one of them have to change their name? This battle seems to rumble on and on for years. Of course, we all want the cuddly panda to win, don't we? But this is trademark law, and even the law of the jungle doesn't always apply.

So what can you do to rescue yourself from this kind of legal trauma? Well, you need to do what you can to reassure yourself (and the lawyers) that you won't be treading on anyone else's trademark toes (or the WWF's furry trademark paws) before you even try to register your name. You do that through trademark searches. But we all know that lawyers are expensive treats, so you need to be canny about how you use them.

Trademarks work like this. When you register your trademark, you register it in the countries in which you're selling (or might sell, in the future). Of course, that question has got slightly more complex with the advent of the internet; it's become harder to define in which territories products and services are actually being "sold." Does selling items to someone in Hong Kong from a website in France count as just selling in Hong Kong, or in France too, or both? What if you had a trademark conflict in France? Could you claim you were only using yours in Hong Kong? Anyway, you decide where you're going to use your trademark as best you can. You also decide what categories of products and services you want to cover. You can't just get a trademark that covers every type of activity in the world. You have to give a description of what "class" of product or service is involved. That's why Polo mints, the Volkswagen Polo and Polo Ralph Lauren are all able to co-exist. Logically of course, the more territories and trademark classes in which you register your name, the more protection you've got. But you can't just go round registering willy-nilly for everything under the sun; you usually have to prove that you've used the mark in the country and category of product or service after five years. And it's expensive. It costs to register a trademark, so the more ground you've got to cover, the more you pay out. There's no point paying for something you know you're never going to use. And you don't just pay to register the name; if you're going through a very thorough naming process, you pay to search the trademark registers before you even get to registering.

Why do you do that? Well, take the UK. When you lodge an application to register a trademark in the UK, your application's published, and then your competitors (who, if they know what they're about, are monitoring trademark applications to make sure there's nothing they think is too close to one of their own) have six months to object to the trademark you've proposed. If no one does, that's all well and good (and your ownership of the trademark is backdated to the date of your application). But if they successfully object, you're left with no name, and you've lost six months. With the speed of marketing at most organizations, you often don't have six months to sit around twiddling your thumbs, waiting to see what happens. Especially if you have to go back to square one with another name, and another.

The solution is trademark searches. That means getting a trademark lawyer to examine your new name, and the trademarks that already exist, to decide if any of them are likely to raise an objection. That way, you can be fairly sure that once you make your application, no one's going to object, and you can probably risk using your name straight away without too much danger of it being challenged.

Again, cost is a big factor. There are different kinds of searches, of different levels of sophistication. The first is an "identical search." This simply looks to see if any identical trademarks exist to the one you're trying to get. It can be pretty rudimentary; if you were searching the name Kinetic for a new product, an identical search wouldn't pick up trademarks like Kinetik, Kinetiq or Qinetiq (the UK defence technology company), even though they all sound identical, and would be likely to cause you a big problem if you were going to launch something similar. But identical searches are relatively cheap, and a good way of knocking out a good number of names from a big list. You can knock out everything with a really obvious direct conflict. In my experience, up to half of any suggested names get knocked out by identicals.

Of course, it depends which trademark classes you're searching – some are much more crowded than others. The trademark system dates back to the last century but one, so, not surprisingly, wasn't particularly set up to deal with things like e-tailing. Categories covering pharmaceuticals and the internet are notoriously crowded, while there are categories covering only cotton bobbins – OK, that's a bit of an exaggeration – where you'd get whatever trademark you wanted in a flash. Again, you do the searches in the territories in which you'd like to register a trademark. Most trademark registers are national, but there are some funny little quirks. Belgium, the Netherlands and Luxembourg are covered by a single Benelux register (good news for you, because it means two fewer registers to search, and two fewer sets of fees to pay). There's also an odd little beast called the Community Trade Mark register, or CTM. This covers the whole of the European Union and, in theory, over time will replace the registers of the individual EU member states. The problem is that at the moment it just sits alongside them. The good side of that for you is that when you finally get to register your name, you can register it in one place and cover the whole of the EU. The bad side is that while you're still searching, to know if you can use your name in one EU country, you need to search both its national register and the CTM. Twice as much work, and twice as much money.

So you've done your identicals, and kissed goodbye to the half of your names that have become has-beens, falling at the first trademark hurdle. This is where it starts to get complicated, slightly traumatic, and much more expensive. At this point, most people cut down the number of names they're looking at to a more manageable shortlist. That could be from around 5 to 15 depending on how many countries and trademark classes you're trying to register in.

You now put that shortlist into "full" searches. This time, the lawyers are looking for a larger number of signs of potential conflict. Does the name look too much like another name that's already registered? Does it sound too much like another trademark (and this will be different in different territories, because of the different sound systems of different languages)? Even, is it too conceptually similar to another name? That one sounds tenuous, but mobile phone company Orange have challenged other mobile phone operators being called things like Green, arguing that they are so closely associated with the use of a colour as a name in mobile telephony that people on the street would think any competitor named with a colour was something to do with them.

Obviously, at this stage, the trademark lawyer's judgment and, much as it pains to me to say it, expertise really comes into play. They essentially have to judge which way a decision would go if a trademark was challenged. It's a risk assessment exercise. And that's what you're paying for.

The trouble is, because there's so much at stake, these lawyers can be pretty tricky to pin down. Some are very, very cautious, highlighting every possible potential problem with every name. Rarely does any name come through full searches with a clean bill of health. Naturally, some of these problems might be much bigger than others – meaning there's a much greater risk of your name being challenged. The problem is, for you and me, it's very difficult to know which is which. And it's why trademark lawyers can often come across like the villains of the naming piece, finding obstacles to every potential name under the sun.

What's the solution? Well, first of all, find a trademark lawyer who's as close to a normal person as you can. And find a trademark lawyer with a good business head, who will be more likely to say, "Yes, these are both *potential* risks, but this one is much more likely than the other." A judgment like that might just come down to the experience of who owns which trademarks – some big companies are notoriously much more vociferous in protecting their intellectual property than others. The trademark lawyer you want will actually give an opinion, and not just beat around the bush. It's only an opinion, not a guarantee, but it is much more useful. Finally, you want a trademark lawyer with just a bit of a bullish attitude. One who takes the point of view of, "How do I get you the trademark you want?" rather than trying to stop you. There is always usually a way out of a trademark dispute, or pre-empting one they think could arise: co-existence agreements, covering where and for what different trademarks can be used non-competitively, and of course, cold, hard cash. So get a trademark lawyer with a bit of attitude and you're more likely to get your way. If I were trying to suss out a trademark lawyer to see just how hard they would fight to get a name I really liked, I'd be asking them, "So, what's the hardest name you've ever had to clear? And how did you manage to get your hands on it in the end?" Allan Poulter, partner at London legal firm Field Fisher Waterhouse is one of these normal, bullish, business-minded lawyers.

And sometimes, you can reassure yourself with a second opinion. I had one client who didn't like the negativity of one trademark lawyer who told him he couldn't use the name he wanted, and so went off and paid another. The lawyer told him something he was much happier with, he went away greatly reassured, and to this day, touch wood, he's never had a problem with the great name I thought of for him (and of course I'm not going to tell you what it is, because then you'll know on what dodgy trademark ground such a great name is standing).

Because all of this umming and aaahing, full trademark searches are dear, and in deciding how you're going to tackle a search, there's always a trade-off between time and money. The quickest way to do full searches would be to search every name you're interested in, in every territory, simultaneously. But that can be prohibitively expensive. On the other hand, the cheapest way would be (just like the six month wait to see if your trademark application is successful) to search each name, one at a time, in each territory, one at a time. But with each full search taking up to two weeks, that could end up taking you years. So usually the time and money you've got available defines your approach to full searches. In most cases, some kind of "phasing" of searches takes place. You search all the names you're interested in in your most important territory. Then you take the names that survive that first phase of searches and put them into the next phase, maybe the next one or two most important territories. This gradual attrition of your lovely ideas means you never know which of your shortlist will end up surviving. In my experience, there might be one, two or three that come out with a much cleaner bill of health than the others. It also means that when you've got your shortlist of five to fifteen names, you have to be prepared for any of them to be the final name you'll go with (because it might be the only survivor of the battle). Within a list that long, it's only human to have favourites.

But if you can't cope with any one of them being the last name standing from full legals, then you shouldn't put it in the list in the first place.

There is a nightmare scenario. That none of the names survive, even after you've spent tens or even hundreds of thousands of dollars on legal searches. This is the lurking threat behind naming that us namers never like to talk about. Some namers and agencies will guarantee that if it does happen, they'll keep on thinking of names until they get one that does get through. Which is great, and reassuring. But there's no guarantee that you'll like the sort of name they come up with to get through legal searches. And they're very careful not to put an absolute time limit on it, which means you might miss deadlines left, right, and centre. They can never *absolutely* guarantee that you'll get a name for what you need in the time you've got.

If all of this is starting to stress you out, we need to keep things in perspective. In four and a half years of full-time naming, with five to ten projects a month, the nightmare scenario really only happened once. And not surprisingly, it was for the name of a worldwide technology company, a notoriously grim legal brief. But boy, was it a nightmare. In the end, some truly hard-ball legal negotiation got them one of the names from the final shortlist (a name no one really liked, but which no one could find a strong enough objection to, either). It was just about on the right side of not bringing on the lawsuits.

Scary, huh? It is all a bit nerve-wracking (you'll be ringing up your trademark lawyer all the time to see how your favourites are doing in the race), but it will stop you bankrupting your company or getting the sack for never actually launching your swanky new brand.

The legal aspect is the bit that's definitely the side of naming that's least understood by clients, and therefore the most intimidating. And at times, it just seems so completely out of your hands. But there is a great danger of legal starting to lead the process; that people come up with names that will give them an easy legal ride, rather than ones that actually answer a strategic brief, or have a great creative idea lurking in them. Trademark lawyers will always push you into weirder-looking names, because the more unusual (read "freakish") they are, the easier their job is to get them through. And lots of the cold, deathly dull and frankly off-putting names out there – often the corporate names of the 1990s, and the pharmaceutical names of, well, really, just about any time – are like that because the people doing the naming are worrying about what will appeal to the lawyers, rather than what will appeal to the rest of us. Glyn Britton says:

I think clients make the mistake of treating their trademark lawyers' advice as instruction. In my experience, lawyers are naturally cautious people, and their advice needs to be put in the context of what's likely to happen, rather than what could happen. If we followed their advice too literally then all brand names would be unique, but also unpronounceable and mostly graceless. Wolff Olins and their clients must have ignored lots of lawyers' advice when they named an airline Go, but somehow it still worked.

The law is a constraint on the creative process of naming. But we need to see it as a challenge – a spur to greater, more original ideas, not a demon we must all be in thrall to. The lawyers loved the name Orange, because when it was thought up, there was simply nothing in its category that was anything like it. By contrast, they will have hated the name for the airline Go, and struggled like billy-o to find a way of registering it and protecting it. Yet to us, those names feel similar. Both have the Wolff Olins 1990s real word simplicity of powerful ideas. Those ideas are more important than the legal strategy it took to make them work.

11

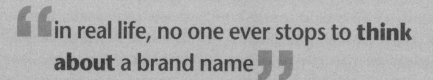

"in real life, no one ever stops to **think about** a brand name**"**

The two-way mirror

SO LET'S SAY A FEW NAMES HAVE MADE IT THROUGH the legal massacre. There is worse to come. I have spent miserable evenings watching people trying to do research into potential names, trying to work out which the public will like.

It's usually been in depressing, middle-England looking homes, somewhere in the commuter belt of London. It will be semi-dark. There will be some lukewarm white wine and some oddly chilled red wine. I will be dropping Marks & Spencer garlic and herb dip on my trousers in the semi-darkness, and wondering if sandwiches are the things that dry out fastest in the entire world. I sit behind a two-way mirror, and on the other side are a group of six people who know we're watching them, but pretending not to, and saying any old nonsense that comes into their heads, safe in the knowledge that all they have to do is talk like a "normal person" convincingly enough for an hour and a half, and then they get £50, which they can go home and spend on Stella or DVDs. And I'd do it too, if anyone would ask me.

Usually when clients asked me about researching names, I gave a vague, noncommittal answer, which was designed to thinly veil my real response, "Don't bother. It's utterly pointless." That might have been a little harsh. It's almost utterly pointless. Of course I could never say that, as the clients had usually invited someone from a research company, who'd come up with a spurious process for researching names, to listen to my answer. The same people who come up with research processes also think up things like nanopeptides in shampoo. Really, we know it just cleans your hair. Really, we know that whatever they say, researchers just ask people what they think.

And in my grumpier moments, I really do question how valuable that is. This sounds like the arrogance of the creative, but there's a bit of truth to it. The Clash sang, "The public wants what the public gets." Henry Ford famously said that if he'd asked his customers what they'd wanted, they'd have said a faster horse. They'd never have come up with the motor car, but of course that's exactly what they did want. If the public were really that good at making the creative leaps of advertising and branding, well they'd be sat the other side of the two-way mirror. Wouldn't they?

It's a situation that is entirely artificial. In real life, no one ever stops to think about a brand name. Occasionally, they might worry about whether they can say the name of a new beer well enough to order one in a bar. But they certainly don't sit there and say, "Hmmm, let me think of all the potential positive and negative connotations of that miserable little word." Think about the last time you walked into Tesco and looked at the name on the cash register. Did the name Siemens send you into fits of Carry-On- Shopping-style giggles? Thought not. Do the first three letters of Coca-Cola embarrass you into

> ## Cillit Bang
>
> I have to say that I'm a late convert to this name. It's a household cleaner, which has been heavily advertised on the telly. It's a name that became famous through people saying, "Where the heck has that come from? What does it mean?" It definitely treads a line between horror and genius, but I've recently decided it's great. It really stands out from its competitors, and has imprinted itself on people's brains with its very weirdness.

dropping the can and running from the corner shop? Exactly. But in research groups, we ask people to imagine every possible problem with every name, however implausible, and obligingly (50 quid in mind) they do it.

In fact, the artificiality of the research situation is highlighted by recent research in *New Scientist* that proves that our brains actually process brand names differently to other everyday words, and to people's names. The process of recognizing brand names seems to involve more of the right side of the brain than for other words. In one sense, that's not surprising. After all, the right side of the brain is often thought of as the more emotional, creative, artistic side. It seems brand names really do carry powerful emotional associations, which is great news for the marketeers of the world. Interestingly, for the designers those marketeers employ, in the same study, brand names were more easily recognized in capital letters. The researchers also noted that brand names are often seen represented in the same way – in a consistent colour or typeface – which could contribute to the different way in which our brains deal with them.

Which is why it's ridiculous to sit in a research group and show people names in black Times New Roman characters on white boards. It's not a realistic representation of how names are encountered and considered in real life (assuming we consciously consider them at all). At the very least, names in research groups should be presented in some kind of plausible context to help punters understand how the names are going to be used, just as I've suggested for client presentations. Show them the names as logos. Show them straplines that might explain how the name will be used. Heck, show them advertising ideas if you can. They all contribute to getting you a more realistic read on how a name will go down.

But even if you do that, in my experience, punters rarely pick the best name. They pick the safest, least offensive name. A risky name is too easy to react against. When Interbrand were researching the name for a new range of biscuits from McVitie's, they investigated two names – HobNobs and OatyWheaty-Crunchies. Now, at that time in the UK, most biscuit brands were named incredibly descriptively – chocolate ginger crunch and so on. Not surprisingly, OatyWheatyCrunchies fared best in research. The public knew exactly what they were getting, and it conformed to all the rules they knew about what biscuits were called. They thought HobNobs was just a bit odd. HobNobs, of course, was trying to do something completely different. It was trying to conjure up less obvious associations: the idea of "hobnobbing" with posh people and a name that simultaneously raised a smile and sent itself up ever so slightly (though when the range was launched, they cleverly emphasized the "nobbliness" of the biscuit, highlighting a more prosaic product feature that was implicit in the name).

On the basis of these research results, McVitie's took an inspired decision. They decided not to go for the safe option. They realized that the public wasn't responding to HobNobs because it was a category breaker – it wasn't playing by the rules of the competitors' names. So, they took a risk, and they went for it. And in time, the fact that it was a name – and a brand – with oodles more personality than any rival biscuit, took it to number one in the category. Likewise, when British Airways created Go the marketing director at the time, David Magliano, said if they'd researched the name, no one would have gone for it.

So is name research good for nothing? Not quite. I'd use it as a "disaster check" – use it to weed out any names that have really significant, negative connotations that the marketing team would never have thought of. That might be particularly important if you're aiming a product at a group of people who are very different to the people thinking of the name, or deciding on it – because they're much younger, older, have different attitudes, or whatever. But once you've used the public to oust any clangers you might have dropped, stop listening. They'll only scare you into picking an easy option.

12

"think of names like the **big nose** or **wide mouth** that every member of the family ends up with"

One of the crowd

if you're only coming up with one name, but what if you've got a whole group of them? In talking about naming strategy, one of the questions I've said you need to ask is whether those names are part of a family. But how do families of names work? How do you know if you've got one? This takes us into the ever so slightly technical territory of what gets variously (and pretentiously) called "naming architecture," "naming hierarchy," or even "nomenclature systems" by Americans. These are naturally all ways of dressing up something relatively straightforward into something more complicated, thus justifying the exorbitant fees of consultants. It's just about a simple system, really. A system of names.

Naming systems depend on two things. First, the strategy of your brand (particularly with regard to, yes, you've guessed it, brand architecture) and the amount of money you've got to spend. How you design your naming system usually falls out of these. The main question that brand architecture helps you to answer is this: what is the role of the different elements of your brand portfolio?

Let's take a classic "monolithic" brand architecture. This means there is one main brand, and everything else is relatively unimportant. BMW is a great example. Most of their marketing effort goes into marketing the BMW brand above all else. Of course, they do market their individual models, most notably the 3, 5, and 7 series. But whether you see an advert for the 3 or 7 series, the spirit of the message is broadly the same. While individual features of the models might be emphasized, they're tied back to the idea that lurks behind everything BMW does, which is something about "superior engineering," expressed in the UK through the strapline, "The ultimate driving machine." So BMW is really the hero. That's where all the emotional communication is done. That checkerboard badge is where they want me to invest my trust, my loyalty, and even my love.

What does that mean for the naming system that goes with it? Well, if BMW is the hero, there needs to be nothing else in the system that "competes" with it. Typically with a monolithic brand, it means the names sitting underneath the master brand are very, very functional: they are often completely descriptive, or alphanumeric as they are in the BMW case. They don't promote the names per se, so the names aren't meant to be exciting. They are there to help you navigate a portfolio of options once they've got us hooked with their main brand. They are usually quite logical (so the 7 Series is bigger than the 5, which is bigger than the 3) but deliberately fairly dull and characterless. As it happens, BMW's 3, 5, and 7 series (or Mercedes-Benz's A, B, or C Class) have probably acquired a little equity of their own, merely through consistent use and people's appreciation of those particular models.

IBM recently invested in rationalizing many of their product names so that IBM was the hero, and most other names became entirely descriptive. Not only did it fit their brand strategy, but also it apparently saved them quite a lot of money. As soon as you decide you are going to name things descriptively, you don't have to spend money creating, searching, registering and protecting potential new names, because they're no longer that important in the scheme of things.

This type of naming architecture works well if your master brand is likely to appeal to all of your potential customers. Arguably, BMW buyers are interested in the same things whether they're buying a 3 or a 7; maybe they're just at different stages of their lives, or have different amounts of money to spend. But if you have products that are marketed at different types of people, with different needs, you might decide that your parent brand is not quite as good at "stretching" its appeal across all of that range. In that case, you might decide to give its products more of a personality of their own; by building more emotion into those products, they're more likely to appeal to their target audiences. And unsurprisingly, in this system, products often function more like sub-brands. Take Ford. They're a big mainstream brand with a wide range of sizes of models, and a wide range of customers. While their customers are probably buying into some aspect of "Fordiness" – its heritage, its reputation for good value, and so on – at either end of its portfolio people are looking for very different qualities. Think of the mum nipping to the shops in her wee supermini, versus the executive in his top of the range saloon. So Ford give names to each of their models to carry a little of that spirit. In Europe, the range looks like this: Ka, Fiesta, Fusion, Focus, C-Max, Mondeo, Galaxy.

This set of names is typical of lots of sub-branded architectures. The names might have a little in common (the initial Fs of Fiesta, Fusion, Focus, or the slight space-ageiness of Galaxy and the recently-retired Scorpio) but don't feel completely like a family. This is probably because the system (or non-system) has probably evolved slowly over time, especially in the world of cars, where the lead-time before new models appear is notoriously long. Some of the names may have been chosen to echo their siblings (I know Fusion was liked partly because it felt right alongside Focus) but there are some glaring anomalies – like the techy-sounding C-Max, or the made up Ka and Mondeo. Does it matter? Well, it won't make or break the company, or the individual models, let's be honest. But a product naming system can bring some consistency and cohesion to a set that can otherwise look random and unrelated. Think of them like the big nose or wide mouth that every member of a family ends up with. You know they're different, but there's some kind of beauty in the fact that there is something which recognizably unites them. That's what a naming system can do.

Car brands are in fact notoriously bad for finding themselves almost on the cusp of a satisfyingly consistent family, and then screwing it up at the last minute. For years, Fiat had been on to a good thing with a set of names which had two features in common: they were real Italian words, that ended in "o": Cinquecento, Uno, Punto, Bravo (admittedly Cinquecento and Uno are numbers to Italian ears; 500 and 1 respectively). But they did feel united. Until along came the Ulysse (pronounced Oo-leese-ay). Now Ulysse is a perfectly good name in its own right, and worked well for the model, which was an MPV. The image of Ulysses on his great voyages in a 5 door Italian bus wasn't all that bad. But amongst its brothers and sisters it just looks a bit odd. Or look at GM's cars in Europe, marketed under the Opal and Vauxhall brands: Agila, Corsa, Meriva, Astra, Vectra. OK, they're not great names, but they work together. Lots of Vs, and final As, and nearly all invented names based on common European scientific vocabulary. It all made quite a lot of sense until the hulking great Signum came along.

This is also a matter of linguistic "territory." You can "own" a style of name – or even a letter – that helps to make your brand more distinctive. For years, Citroën "owned" the letter X. First in alphanumeric names like CX, BX and XM, and then in made up words using initial Xs, like Xsara and Xantia. These slightly unusual looking creations absolutely fitted with the slight air of unapologetic eccentricity that Citroëns (and Citroën owners) cultivated for years. Other car marques naturally avoided the Citroën X. They don't seem to know what they've thrown away by moving to C3s and C5s.

It's not surprising that this linguistic territory often coincides with real geographical territory. The Fiat names make sense to us because they reflect the brand's Italian heritage. One of my favourite naming systems is that for Ikea's furniture, where everything gets a Swedish name and a functional description. While I don't know what the Swedish names mean, they reinforce Ikea's Scandinavian cool, have a little bit of mystery about them, and are really distinctive.

What constitutes the link in naming systems can be quite subtle. Orange's product and service names in the UK really just have in common that they're all real words written with capital letters. But it means they don't have any names that are glaringly inconsistent. The UK mobile phone brand One2One (which has since been bought by Deutsche Telekom and rebranded T-Mobile) used to follow the pattern of the main brand with nearly every product name they had, leading to names like Less2Pay and More2Say. Really consistent, and really recognizable, but it seemed like it was getting harder and harder for them to find names that fitted the pattern. They were probably delighted when they were bought out. Though T-Mobile have continued with the spirit with product names that reflect their own name, like T-Zones and U-Fix.

Of course, some architecture means you can throw all the rules out of the window. If your products, or target audiences, are so different from one another that you think there's nothing you can find in common that will appeal to them all, then you can afford to give them all names that are completely unrelated. This is the "freestanding" or "house of brands" approach. Think of the huge conglomerates like Procter & Gamble or Unilever. They own brands like Dove, Lynx, Persil, Bird's Eye and Wall's, all sitting alongside each other. But they don't think it helps them to link those names together, so they don't. Of course, on paper that's a costly approach (indeed, Unilever is the second highest spender on advertising in the UK, after the Government) but it means each one of those brands needs to be marketed and promoted separately. But they think the costs are worth it to sell each of those individual brands.

These three styles of architecture are usually just textbook examples, though. In real life, the nature of business, with people coming and going in jobs after relatively short periods of time, each desperate to make a lasting mark, means most real brand portfolios are a jumble of all three. Few people really maintain the admirable long-term vision in the face of short-term goals. And so most naming portfolios are a right old hodge-podge too. They have a mixture of all sorts of different types.

Now that's not necessarily a problem, as long as you know why you were doing it. As we've seen, those decisions should be the product of a bit of logic. The good thing about a naming system is that it can provide you with a structure for that logical thinking. So, question one: what's the purpose of what you're naming? Is it just a navigational part of your structure? If so, it makes sense to give it a purely functional name. If not, what message or personality should it be putting across that the main brand isn't? And if you pick a name with bags of personality, which isn't that descriptive, do you have the money to support it? If not, it should probably go back down the duller end of the naming spectrum. This kind of logic should stop you ending up with a car whose name contains a long string of confusing metaphors but no real information. That's not to say that names at the descriptive, functional end of the spectrum have to be really boring. That depends on the brand's tone of voice – the sort of language that it uses to explain things. Is your brand the sort that might talk about a Small Handled Hot Liquid Receptacle, or would you just call it a teacup? I worked with a utility company who wanted to find a better way of referring to their "prepay" service, essentially for people they thought might default on their payments. We could have just called it Prepay – probably a perfectly good name that their customers would have understood. But we decided to think of a more positive way of thinking of it, while still being descriptive. The company already had a successful product called One Bill, so the answer seemed obvious. Prepay became No Bill. Still descriptive, but much more interesting.

When I talk about naming systems, people's desire to name every possible thing kicks in. Perhaps it's an instinct to leave our mark wherever we go. Alongside actual names of products and services – the things punters can actually buy – companies are always naming categories of things, initiatives, promotions, internal stuff. I often think of these more as "labels" than names. I tend to be quite strict with people about what needs a "name" and what doesn't. There are lots of things that really don't need names in their own right; we can just describe things in everyday language, and that will be less confusing. Typically, a good rule of thumb is to only spend time thinking of names for things that you want customers to use or remember – things they might go into a shop and ask for, ring you about, or mention to their friends. If you don't want to do that, you're probably better off doing something else. Like going home for the night.

13

"the best answer might be staring you in the face**"**

Put up or shut up

Now the time has come to put my naming where my mouth is; to talk about some of the names I've been involved in, and talk about where they came from – what the brief was, and how we answered it. Then you can decide if me and my book are really just all talk and no action.

Ocado

Ocado is an on-line supermarket in the UK. Now it's backed by the high street retailer the John Lewis Partnership (through their supermarket subsidiary called Waitrose), but when we were naming it, it was a mere dot com start-up, set up by some very bright young lads who'd left Goldman Sachs to do it. Right from the start, they decided to do things properly, managing to poach some high-flying food retailers from Marks & Spencer (whose wealthy customers were exactly the type they were aiming for). And as part of doing things properly, branding came very high on their list of things to think about early. They thought about it right from the off, and now have Interbrand's chief executive on board to make sure they keep thinking about it.

Their idea was to make their brand about "supermarket shopping the way it should be." By taking orders on the internet, and then supplying the orders from a warehouse, they could more reliably keep track of what they had in stock, and actually supply what people wanted – different from the other supermarkets, which were still then largely fulfilling their orders from their shops. That made it harder for them to know exactly what they had on the shelves, and you would occasionally find yourself ordering a pineapple, but when the little man in the van came round, they'd often run out of pineapples so gave you a bag of carrots instead. Not much cop.

So the new brand had to stand in opposition to the traditional supermarkets. As we've seen, most UK retailers are named after their founders. The names often have a possessive "s" at the end (or one that now merges into the name) – Sainsbury's, Selfridges, Woolworth's – or were given one even when the names weren't actually surnames. So the first part of the brief was to come up with something that didn't sound like a person.

There were two big defining constraints on the naming brief. First, we were coming up with the name at the height of the dot com boom, and the company were adamant that their domain name should be a dot com, and ideally the brand name would be exactly the same as the URL. Since at that time nearly every real English word had been registered as a dot com (and trying to buy them was typically costing an arm and a leg), we knew we were probably looking for a made-up name.

The third constraint was down to a strategic question. At the time of naming, e-tailing was just getting off the ground. There was no problem, in the customers' eyes, with someone delivering pre-packed items like toilet rolls and tins of beans. But there were very few brands they trusted to pick fresh things like fruit and veg for them. The perception was that without being there in person to pick up a nice looking fruit, the supermarkets would just scrape the bottom of the barrel (maybe literally) and send it over in a mucky Transit van. Of course the real, germladen truth is quite different. Apparently every apple we buy in a normal supermarket has already been handled by nearly twenty sweaty-pawed punters like ourselves. By contrast, order it on the internet, and it probably gets touched by one or two at most, so it ends up being much more hygienic. But that's not what the public thought. Research showed there were two UK food retailers they would trust to choose decent produce on their behalf: Marks & Spencer, and, not surprisingly, Waitrose – who subsequently saw the congruence between their own brand and the new one and bought a stake. But at the time, we didn't have the advantage of the Waitrose name to drop and assuage people's fruit-based phobias.

So we decided that to help reassure people, the name should be based around the language of fresh fruit and vegetables, to reinforce their freshness credentials. Knowing we probably wouldn't get our hands on the dot coms of their real names (especially given the virtual fruit bowl of names for technology companies out there – think Orange, Apple, BlackBerry, Apricot) we needed to play around with them (although we actually came quite close to using the name Sugarsnap – the British English name for snowpeas). That meant topping and tailing the names like you might a green bean, or mixing the ingredients of their names. So we came up with the likes of Fruitpassion and Beanrunner. (I still think it should have been called that, given that they actually run your shopping round to your door. But they thought it sounded too down-market.) So Ocado, as lots of people have suspected, is just the word "avocado" with its top lopped off (and that's usually my short version of the Ocado story). We liked its balanced, almost symmetrical look, its shortness, and the fact that it lent itself really nicely to design work. John Holton, the very talented designer who came up with the concept (now at brand consultants Figtree), designed a logo that echoed the round characters of the initial O and C, and also suggested a fruit being peeled. Set against a backdrop of the rich, beautiful colours and textures of more fruit and veg (a technique lots of the other retailers have since copied left, right, and centre), the implied freshness of their stuff was reinforced even further.

Since the brand has launched, two problems have raised their heads. First, it was beaten to market just slightly by travel brand Opodo, started as a joint venture between a number of airlines. The names look and sound similar, and are both online, so not surprisingly lots of people confuse the two (although I still think Ocado is a much better name than Opodo, which seems to be completely meaningless, and bears no relation to the concept it's selling).

Secondly, while Ocado is short, it's not that easy to spell (if you've only heard the name) or pronounce (if you've only seen it written down). It could be written Ohcahdoh, Ocardo (if you're a posh Southern Brit, which most of its customers are) and many more ways besides. It could be said Oca-DOO, O-CAY-do, OCK-ad and many more ways besides. Of course, it's all very simple if you pick up on its avocado-based origins, but it's just a wee bit too subtle. So the company, being, like I said, quite sharp cookies, have taken to radio ads that spell out the name: O, C, A, D, O, Ocado.com. The tune is awful, but does its job. And a good example of how you can get the rest of your marketing and communications to make up for the shortcomings of your name. Although when I went on the radio the other week, and talked about Ocado, of course innocent old me got the blame for the irritating jingle.

Jetix

Jetix is one of those names that look like it has just landed from another planet. Which was sort of the plan. Jetix is the new name for the Fox Kids TV channel. Now, why would you change the name of something as successful and well-known as that? Well, the big problem was that Fox TV sold it to Disney. Suddenly the Fox in the name looked a bit odd. It would have been easy just to somehow rename the thing in line with some of Disney's other brands. But Fox Kids didn't quite fit with the rest of Disney's portfolio, or more importantly with the Disney brand.

The Disney brand is all about wholesome family entertainment. The sort of thing a group of well-fed, white-teethed, middle class families all sit down and watch together. They have fun, and learn some valuable lessons about life along the way (cynical, moi?). But Disney own lots of things that don't always fit so snugly with that sunshiny, butter-wouldn't-melt view of the world, so they're quite careful not to use the Disney name for those sorts of things: like the ABC TV channel in the states, or Miramax films. Fox Kids was one of those exceptions to the rule, too. Although it's children's TV, it's of quite a different character to that of Disney's. Where Disney TV is exactly what mums and dads want their little pride and joy to watch, Fox Kids teeters on the edge of parental disapproval. Not what they'd switch off, but definitely programmes focused on the kids and not the family. In fact, that's why Disney wanted to buy Fox Kids, because they were covering a whole group of kids that wouldn't be interested in Mickey's big ears. So they bought it and the Fox had to be culled.

What to replace it with? Disney were of course worried that if the name just changed to something unfamiliar, or worse, unrecognizable, then kids would just desert the channel. So they needed the new name to be as easy to introduce as possible. The first part of the brief was that the X of Fox Kids was quite a prominent part of the channel's logo, made up of two criss-crossing cartoon versions of the searchlights we know from the 20th Century Fox film intros. So here was Disney's first canny move. While they weren't allowed to keep the original X, they wanted a name with an X in it, ideally at the end, so they could make something of a subliminal connection with the old, successful, popular name.

The core of the Fox Kids audience were 8-year-old boys, so we were looking for something that would appeal to them. We wanted to play on the sense of fantasy and adventure in Fox's cartoons, and capture in the name some of the slightly manic energy of the channel and its contents. Kids are very accepting of new, odd names: think about the crazy names of Lord of the Rings, or Harry Potter, or Pokémon. In fact Pokémon is a stalwart of the Fox Kids schedule. But kids do like names to be easy to say, so we were looking for something, which had a simple consonant-vowel-consonant-vowel structure (that would also help the name be easy to pronounce across the world, since Fox Kids is a big global operation). We were also chopping up words that felt right, like "energy" and "energetic." And it's from the latter that Jetix was created, with the J at the beginning making it look more distinctive, and giving a nice link to "jet." We added the final X from the brief, which also gives the name that bit of a sci-fi edge. It's the sort of name that looks really quite odd to us fuddy-duddy grown-ups, but seems to work a treat with the littl'uns. Naturally this all sounds rather astonishingly well-rationalized. Of course, when you come up with a name, you are not consciously trying to achieve all of that at the same time – you'd numb your brain until it couldn't do anything. But the magic of naming is that without thinking too hard you can come up with things which subconsciously communicate quite a lot.

Then, Disney made another canny move to help them implement the name. Before the channel ultimately changed its name, they began a strand of programming on the then Fox Kids channel called Jetix, and trailed it heavily on their website, which was a big part of the Fox experience. That way they got their audience used to the new name, before it really took hold. So when it was finally changed for good, it was much less of a surprise, and kids were much less likely to be bamboozled and go channel-hopping.

Intelligent Life

The Economist is a very respected magazine. It is famed for its ability to present serious and complex business and political issues in an accessible way, without dumbing down. In fact, the style guide it gives to its journalists, to help them write its way, has even become a bit of a legend in itself, used by other journalists and businesspeople the world over. Not only that, but *The Economist*'s advertising is revered in the UK for its witty and erudite style, usually entirely based on words written in white on a red background. The advertising itself has become so famous that you can buy attractive coffee-table books full of its posters. Sometimes, so recognizable have they become, *The Economist* name doesn't even appear on the ad. My favourite is the one that says:

I never read *The Economist*.
(Management trainee, 42)

So you can imagine that coming up with a name for *The Economist* means more than a little pressure on a lowly namer.

You see, *The Economist* doesn't just produce their weekly magazine. They also produce what they call "annuals," thicker, glossier (and naturally more expensive) books that come out once a year, and which are the perfect thing for high-flying international businessmen to pick up in the business class lounge and read on the plane, between sips of gin and tonic and really, really salty salted peanuts. When they came to us, they had one annual called "The World In... " followed by the number of the coming year. It comes out around Christmas time to give these business types something to read so they don't have to talk to their families over the holiday season. Because it did so well, *The Economist* was looking for a summer equivalent.

The new annual was not going to be the usual economic and political digest. Instead it was going to talk about "lifestyle" trends – gadgets, holidays, wellbeing, you know the stuff. It was designed to give *The Economist* treatment to the other side of business people's lives. So it needed a name that hinted that it was about more than you'd usually expect of *The Economist*, but that it would be done in the same inimitable style. The name had to have a bit of class, to live up to the all-conquering tone set by the advertising. Enter *Intelligent Life*. It suggested "lifestyle" and how they were going to treat it, as well as being an already-existing phrase, as in, "Is there intelligent life on other planets?" That helps make it more memorable and it also managed ever so slightly to flatter the reader into thinking they were living the intelligent life, just by buying a few shiny pages. I think it's a great name, and we were really chuffed with it. It seems to have done the trick. *Intelligent Life* is selling well, and there are rumours that it might become a more regular fixture on the newsstands than the current yearly visitor.

Teleport

"Video on demand" is an exciting idea. Tell your TV what you want to watch – the edition of *The Office* that was on two weeks ago, tonight's *Doctor Who*, or anything with Jamie Oliver in, say – and it'll get it for you. It's like having the best video shop in the world round the corner (oh and the TV archives), without you ever having to leave your seat. Couch potato heaven.

So an exciting idea, but not that exciting a name. "Video on demand" is exactly the sort of name that techies and product managers come up with. It's a really good description of how the technology works, but it never really gets the juices flowing. Yet often in emerging technological domains, the techies christen it, journalists pick up on it, and pretty soon, it becomes the standard. Only occasionally can you ever reverse it. Mobile phone brand Orange famously did just that, when they wanted to promote SMS services. They realized that another techy set of initials (which stand for "short message service") couldn't adequately communicate what this new technology even was, let alone did. So Orange decided to translate "SMS" into something that ordinary people might get. "Text message" was the result, and now texting is in the dictionary (although oddly, Nokia were one of the slowest to catch on – it's only recently made it into the dictionary on their phones). Unfortunately for

Orange, because "text message" is so descriptive of the product, they're not able to trademark it, own it, and really get the credit for the translation they did. But I'm sure it's no coincidence that us Brits are some of the biggest users of SMS, and also the ones who don't call it that.

So the UK cable TV company Telewest wanted to do the same for video on demand, only this time they wanted something ownable. We looked at metaphors for things that seemed to miraculously take you wherever you wanted to go (like to Ramsay Street for example, if that's what you fancy). A magic carpet seeming a little bit too low-tech, we plumped for Teleport, the sci-fi device that zapped you across the universe at the touch of a button. It was a nice metaphor, with a nice futuristic edge to it, without it being too scary and technical, and what's more, there was even a nice echo of Telewest at the beginning to remind you who was behind this great new bit of kit.

Marksmith

Good one, this. It shows how naming needn't take you months, and how the best answer might be staring you in the face. A designer friend of mine was setting up his own business, and needed a name for his company. He rang me from the steps of Companies House, having been about to go in with his name just as it was. But at the last minute, a crisis of confidence: was it too similar to the names of other people? Was that too boring? What if his newly-fledged company grew into the corporate giant he hoped, and his name alone felt like a vanity project, or just too limiting? We only had a couple of minutes to think about it, so we had to come up with something quick. His name? Mark Smith. There are a lot of them about. But we were thinking about what he does; at its simplest, he makes marks that help identify brands. Trademarks, in fact. What might he have been called in medieval times, the times of blacksmiths and locksmiths? Why, a marksmith. It seemed perfect. A name that is descriptive, makes a story of the founder, and feels clever, imaginative and traditional all at the same time. A bobby dazzler, that one.

BrightHouse

This is a British retailer close to my heart, mainly because there's a branch of it in the Elephant and Castle shopping centre, just around the corner from my house (until the nasty old Elephant gets knocked down that is). It means that if I'd come up with a horrible name for the thing I'd have had to face it nearly every day.

BrightHouse used to be called Crazy George's. I know. For some reason they'd gone for an American theme, even at one point using a kind of Uncle Sam figure on their marketing materials, who was presumably Crazy George himself. But the name wasn't doing it any favours. For they sold household stuff like furniture and hi-fis to people who wouldn't normally get credit. Their interest rate is quite high to reflect that risk. So all in all, Crazy George's was sending an odd message. They even did some research into their name, which ended up seeming to suggest, "You'd have to be crazy to give me credit," or perhaps, "I'd have to be crazy to pay that much."

The brief was to find something a little softer. We also thought it would be nice to think of Crazy George's as "the exception to the rule," leading to ideas for names like Treefrog – the frog that lives in a tree! But coupled with an amazingly brightly coloured, bug-eyed frog logo, oddly the client just wasn't biting. So the slightly more conservative BrightHouse was chosen. It hit the mark because it coincided with a rash of home improvement shows on the TV, and did that favourite old namer's trick – rhyming with a much more well-known word or phrase (lighthouse, in this case, obviously) to make it more memorable.

Eurosource

Ah, the name that got away. Two political publishers – Dod's in the UK (authors of the revered *Dod's Parliamentary Companion*) and the brilliantly named Le Trombinoscope in France – were coming together to produce a guide to the members of the European Parliament, and the way it worked. Now this great tome needed a name that would work across all the rapidly escalating number of member states. Given that it was the only product of its ilk in its field, I and my partners on the project, design and branding consultancy R&D&Co, felt we could afford to take a few risks. Strangely, these kinds of reference compendia typically have quite unusual names – think of *Debrett's* guide to etiquette; *Jane's Defence Weekly* (who the heck is this Jane? Why is she so interested in tanks?); even the old but quirkily monikered *Who's Who*. We wanted something with this sort of unexplained authority, something that would resonate in all of these countries because it wasn't too literal. We were thinking of names like Orpheus (with the nice EU in the middle). We could hear Strasbourg mandarins saying, "Oh my word, I must look her up in Orpheus." We even toyed with making the book bright pink, so it would stand out from the other dusty grey volumes on the civil servants' shelves, and calling it just Magenta (that's one of the words which looks and feels the same in lots of languages), as in, "What does Magenta have to say on the matter?"

Alas it wasn't to be. It was a little bold for Dod's and Le Trombinoscope. So Eurosource it was. Fine, but not the character it could have been.

Crocus

The story of Crocus is the sort of story that makes us namers look complete frauds. But I can't claim the credit for this one. That belongs to my friend Lou Dawson of Attention Seekers, a former colleague at Interbrand and a former European marketing director for Hurley International, a clothing brand owned by Nike (as all the supercool skaters and surfers reading this book will be able to testify).

Lou took a call from a potential new client, who explained that they were building what they hoped would become the number one gardening retail website in the UK. Lou explained how a naming process might work, how much it would cost, how long it would take, and how they needed to be clear on their naming strategy. Lou said, "Are you thinking of a made-up name, like Kodak, or the name of something related, which already exists, like, I don't know, Crocus?"

The client bought our proposal, and we did our usual two rounds of naming ideas. But one name just wouldn't disappear from everyone's thoughts. It just felt right. And despite the fact that this naming job took place in the middle of the dot com boom, incredibly they managed to get their hands on the domain they wanted. So Crocus.co.uk was born, named in about twenty seconds during the first ever conversation about the brief.

Fusion

I nearly got my own example like that, working on the name for a Ford small utility vehicle in Europe. We'd just walked through Ford's factory, with people frantically throwing dustsheets over confidential designs we weren't supposed to see as we walked past, to get our first brief on the name. Everything they told us suggested that the car's name should suggest a coming together of two things – a practical small car, plus something more rugged and roomy. Plus Ford liked the alliteration of names that started with F (think Focus, and Fiesta), as well as names which had a hint of popular science about them. *Surely* this should be called the Fusion, shouldn't it? I asked. It was greeted with groans. Everyone agreed that Fusion would be a great name, and that Ford even already owned the trademark, but that the Ford high command had already earmarked it for another model. So off we went, did our homework, our two rounds of naming, legal and linguistic searches, and ate our Ford meeting biscuits (as signed for by the vice-president of marketing). And eighteen months later, what should roll on to the streets but the real version of the fibreglass model I'd seen in Dagenham, with a little badge on the back saying "Fusion." The moral of the story is it's worth knowing which names you really can use and which you can't before you spend cash on the consultants.

I did learn a valuable lesson from Ford though. They told me that when they were presenting names to Ford's then worldwide boss, Jac Nasser, they always presented him with two options (so he could exercise the 50 per cent naming rejection rule). One was the one they wanted, and one was so terrible they were certain he'd never pick it. And luckily it seems he never did. He went away feeling he'd made a crucial executive decision, and they got their way.

14

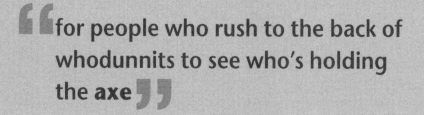

" for people who rush to the back of whodunnits to see who's holding the **axe "**

The secret rules
of naming

SO THERE THEY WERE. The perils of naming products, companies and brands. Hopefully my cunning branding wiles have persuaded you that it's all so much more complicated than you thought. Or maybe, that the bits you thought would be easy are harder than they look, and the tough bits are actually quite easy.

So what have we learnt? Well, that there are some secret rules of naming, the rules you need to have done a lot of naming (and seen lots of projects go awry, if not completely pear-shaped) to really appreciate. So, this bit is for people who rush to the back of whodunnits to see who was holding the axe. This is the end of our quest – the rules themselves. Here they are, all laid out for you in black and white, a cut-out-and-keep guide to the 22 commandments of naming to save you the hassle of your project being the one that goes completely off the rails.

You don't have to follow all of them, but each one should at least give you something to think about. Good luck. Hopefully, you'll end up with an Orange or a Häagen-Dazs, and not a Grazia or a Bravia, two shocking new names for a magazine and TV. But can you tell which one's which?

1. Define the brief as precisely as you can

Which countries are you going to need a name in?

What trademark classes are you looking at?

Does the name need to fit in a family of names?

What territory do the competitors own (and can you do the opposite)?

What's the most important thing for the name to say?

Do you need a domain name? If so, are you prepared to buy one?

2. Decide what type of name you need

This will usually depend on how much money you've got to spend on it and where it's got to work.

3. Check what names your company might already own, but isn't using

4. Don't allow too much time for the process

Naming works best with a bit of pressure, so people are forced to come up with names quickly and instinctively, and decisions are made without interminable months of pointless soul-searching.

5. Run a competition internally to come up with names

They might come up with something good (and save you the expense of employing someone expensive like me). But even if they come up with rubbish, it'll help you later on.

6. Get people in a room to think up names

... especially the key decision makers, so that they'll feel involved (and realize it's not as easy as they think).

7. If you need to, get someone good with words to have a few ideas too

8. Get the key decision makers together

Get them to look at a first lot of names, and decide what sort of names are working and which aren't.

9. Go away and think of more, on the basis of the feedback

10. Whittle all the names down to a shortlist

Then present it to the key decision makers.

11. Present names in some kind of context

Don't just show them as words in black and white on the page. Turn them into logos, or put them on business cards or in newspaper headlines. Try a strapline or two that helps the names along.

12. Whittle all the names down to an even shorter shortlist

Do this with your key decision makers. This time, make sure that every name on the list is one that you'd happily launch, if it came to it. This really is crunch time. There's no room for wobbles later.

13. Buy the domain names of any names on your short shortlist that aren't registered

It's cheap, and boy, will you kick yourself if they've gone by the time you get to the end of the process. I mean *really* kick yourself.

14. Do a linguistic check on your short shortlist

And then throw out anything that's got a big language problem in an important market.

15. Do legal searches on all the names left on your short shortlist

Ask your lawyer what it would take to get you each name (not what the problems are with each name, or you'll never get anything).

16. If you absolutely must, do some research with punters

But only if you've got more than one name left at the end of the process. Present the names in context and not just as names on bits of card. Only rule out a name on the basis of their feedback if a name has a cut and dried negative. Ignore any more equivocal feedback. Most of them don't know what they're talking about. That's why you're doing your job and they're not. It's up to you to make it work.

17. Handling the big boss

If you have a big boss thousands of miles away who insists on having a say at this unhelpful point, don't just tell them the name. Ideally take them through the whole story, and ideally try the Jac Nasser trick. Give them a choice between the name you want them to go for, and something so terrible they'd never choose it in a thousand years.*

18. Give the name a logo, a strapline, an ad campaign

… anything it needs to make it work.

19. Get your story straight

Make sure you have a convincing answer to "Why is it called that?" or "Where did the name come from?" The best answer to the latter question is, "From our internal competition." Even if it's not true.

20. Tell your staff about the name first

Tell them the answers to rule 19 – for when the press asks them.

21. Tell the rest of the world what the new name is

Always tell them your answers to rule 19 as well, until you've bored yourself half to death.

*and just don't blame me if they choose the one that's obviously terrible.

22. Stick to your guns

Whatever the press or the public say, don't wobble. They'll get used to it. But if they smell your fear, they'll be merciless.

There you go. Easy. Just don't tell the consultants I told you.

About the author

Neil Taylor is an expert on brands, and how they use language. He's creative director of The Writer (www.thewriter.co.uk), and has been described as "the David Beckham of naming" (when that was still good). He's helped clients name everything from supermarkets to TV technology to toilet roll. He was previously a senior naming consultant at global brand consultancy Interbrand.

Most days, he spends his time training people to become better writers at work (when he's not writing the menus for Greek restaurant chains). He works with people like the BBC, Unilever, PricewaterhouseCoopers, Sotheby's and 3.

He's also written *Search Me: The surprising success of Google*, co-edited *From Here to Here: Stories inspired by London's Circle Line*, and is a contributor to *Common Ground: Around Britain in 30 writers* and *26 Letters: Illuminating the alphabet*, also published by Cyan. And he's on the board of business writers' group 26.

Also available from Cyan/Marshall Cavendish

We, Me, Them & It
How to write powerfully for business
John Simmons

"A rarity in the world of business books: something readable, stimulating and full of good sense... Simmons makes a heartfelt plea for plain English, and encourages us to harness the power of words to tell stories, embody corporate ideals, and help to create brands."
Book of the Week, *Marketing* magazine

In other times we might have called it a paean. Today, perhaps, a song of praise to the infinite power of words, a confession of a life-long affair with language.

This is a business book with a difference – a business book that is an intriguingly good read. It's aimed at business people who recognize the need for more creativity at work, and at creative people who are looking for new ways to make a difference to their clients' business performance. It makes an unashamed appeal to our emotional as well as our rational nature, showing the way we can use words to gain competitive advantage in business life.

ISBN-13: 978-1-904879-68-8
ISBN-10: 1-904879-68-3
UK £9.99 • USA $17.95 • CAN $24.95

The Invisible Grail
How brands can use words to engage with audiences
John Simmons

"How to make love, not war, with words. *The Invisible Grail* is absolutely chock full of insight and fresh ideas about brands, business and language."
James Hill, Chairman, Birds Eye Wall's

All brands want to be loved. Creating that positive emotional connection between product and audience is brand management's holy grail. But not all brands achieve this goal. And perhaps the ones that most want to be loved are the ones that fall shortest of finding affections. What are those brands missing? How can they bring themselves closer to their customers and their own people? How can they reveal the grail?

The Invisible Grail is an immensely stimulating book for anyone close to brands. It will take you on a captivating journey of discovery with a valuable treasure awaiting at the end.

ISBN-13: 978-1-904879-69-5
ISBN-10: 1-904879-69-1
UK £9.99 • USA $17.95 • CAN $24.95

Why Entrepreneurs Should Eat Bananas
101 inspirational ideas for growing your business and yourself
Simon Tupman

"This fast-moving book is packed with practical ideas and insights that you can apply immediately to achieve greater profitability in your business."
Brian Tracy, author of *Eat That Frog!*

Are you:
- Working long and exhausting hours?
- Busting a gut over unprofitable customers?
- Reluctant to delegate?
- Lacking in self-confidence to promote your business?
- Wishing there were 30 hours in the day?
- Suffering unhealthy stress levels?
- Not devoting enough time to your family and friends?

In this groundbreaking book, Simon Tupman offers 101 practical ideas to help you become a superstar entrepreneur with a life. You will discover:
- How to stay on top in business in the 21st century.
- How to work smarter, not harder.
- How to attract new business.
- How to bring out the best in your team and free up your time.
- How to promote yourself professionally.
- Ways to keep happy and healthy.

Plus:
- Insights from five entrepreneurs from around the world.

ISBN-13: 978-1-904879-49-7
ISBN-10: 1-904879-49-7
UK £8.99 • USA $16.95 • CAN $22.95